HAUNTED
HARBOR

HAUNTED HARBOR

HARBOR

Charleston's Maritime Ghosts
and the Unexplained

GEORDIE BUXTON & ED MACY

CHARLESTON LONDON
History
PRESS

Published by The History Press
18 Percy Street
Charleston, SC 29403
866.223.5778
www.historypress.net

Cover photo by Claire Kramer.

First published 2005
Manufactured in the United Kingdom
ISBN 1.59629.074.9

Library of Congress Cataloging-in-Publication Data
Buxton, Geordie.
   Haunted harbor : Charleston's maritime ghosts and the unexplained
/ Geordie Buxton and Ed Macy.
     p. cm.
     ISBN 1-59629-074-9 (alk. paper)
   1. Haunted places--South Carolina--Charleston. 2. Ghosts--South
Carolina--Charleston. 3. Charleston (S.C.)--History.   I. Macy, Ed.
II. Title.
BF1472.U6B88 2005
133.1'09757'915--dc22
                    2005016588

Photos of Castle Pinckney copyright March 20, 1968, by Dewey Swain and June 28, 1983, by
W.A. Jordan.
Published with permission by *Post and Courier*.
Other photos by Geordie Buxton, Claire Kramer and Jayson Polansky.

"Tympanum Sea" originally published in *Musings of the Lowcountry Anthology I*, copyright 1997.

The names of some people involved in these stories have been changed either by their request, or
because their relatives have asked us to do so.

Notice: The information in this book is true and complete to the best of our knowledge. It is offered
without guarantee on the part of the author or The History Press. The author and The History
Press disclaim all liability in connection with the use of this book.

"TYMPANUM SEA"
By Geordie Buxton

Underneath the sun, I never got to sleep
beside something true in the silences of dreaming.
These noisy towns drown out those sacred places
nobody may ever hear or see to understand.

In all this shame, I can still find reason for one
simple act of kindness, and let you in, guiding
you through as you step across my threshold.
These storms lift up fast out of the waters

they shake the towns and all of the trees.
A radio is on in my home because the wind,
howling and moaning, and the rain, pounding
are not enough to keep me covered from you.

When the electricity cuts off I light candles
because I am afraid of the dark silences.
Above, circling like whirlpools in a mad sea
are the clouds, lessening and breaking for the sun.

I wish with all my strength for one more drop
to fall and ricochet off the roof in a sonic boom
that will send the entire town out of their homes
and be read in tomorrow's paper by the mayor.

I tire and feel a drunken surrender to dream
of the destination of this last rain drop, singular
and forgotten, blown southwest like a ghost in the wind
as it falls away to a vast sanctuary, the ocean

onto a sun-slashed surface, dispersed, stretched
and sinking down beyond a school of dolphin
breathing water and floating motionless through
the barnacled doorways of a lost civilization

I see this last rain drop, scattering through
another ten thousand leagues of salt water
down to the thick deep blueness of a basin.
Here we are, yourself and every part of me.

Listen…listen. Listen.

To all those who have been swallowed by the sea.

Thanks to Pat Mellen, Adam Artigliere,
Carlin Thomas at Fort Sumter National Park, Harbor Pilot Mohn Stuhr and
Brian Collins of Sandlapper Tours.

Thank you also to the Knoths of Carolina Polo, Jennifer McCurry,
José Hernandez and the Wentworths.

Contents

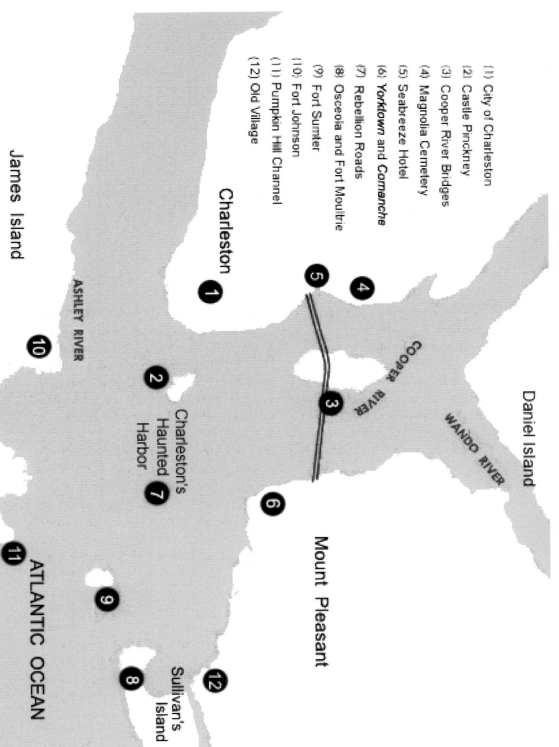

(1) City of Charleston
(2) Castle Pinckney
(3) Cooper River Bridges
(4) Magnolia Cemetery
(5) Seabreeze Hotel
(6) *Yorktown and Comanche*
(7) Rebellion Roads
(8) Osceola and Fort Moultrie
(9) Fort Sumter
(10) Fort Johnson
(11) Pumpkin Hill Channel
(12) Old Village

James Island

Charleston

Daniel Island

ASHLEY RIVER

COOPER RIVER

WANDO RIVER

Charleston's
Haunted
Harbor

Mount Pleasant

ATLANTIC OCEAN

Sullivan's
Island

Introduction

These stories are about the sea and what it has meant to Charleston, South Carolina. In a way, the authors are given extreme license when the theme is the sea, for every bounty on the shore has its roots in the froth. Almost everything can be tied to the sea when your setting is this town. For the sake of avoiding a voluminous calamity of words and images, these are the stories that are the most mysterious, like a wooden bow disappearing into murk, never to exist in the same form again. These are stories of the countless souls who did not get tombstones on the land but instead with the legacy of the tides.

Many moons ago, I boastfully called Charleston "the most haunted city in North America" on worldwide television. It was during the witching season, and I was leading a five-person camera crew from CNN around some of the city's darker alleys, ballast-stone side streets and even a mostly subterranean dungeon by the light of a foul-smelling railroad lantern. These media folk had heard the rumors and stories that surround Charleston and had enlisted me—a self-professed expert on the supernatural underbelly of the city—to be their guide. While we saw none of the city's notorious nocturnal dwellers that October evening, it was clear to all of us that this place has a seriously macabre history—still, could it be the most haunted city in North America?

Since my small-screen debut, I've heard my comment rebuked countless times, especially from people in places like Gettysburg, Pennsylvania; Salem, Massachusetts; and Savannah, Georgia. I don't actually believe there is a way to gauge the supernatural activities of a particular area. Not long ago, I got a call from a gentleman out west who ran a ghost tour from a bus. He proudly exclaimed that he was the possessor of a "ghost finder," an "absolute necessity" on his tours. I weaseled enough information from him to determine this piece of equipment was no more than the meter that electricians use to determine if something is giving off juice. His main selling point was that this thing detected "movement." This sort of technology only exists in the realms of Hollywood—or the very fringes of cutting-edge parapsychology.

Despite what might seem like an overwhelming cynicism toward those who are intent on making ghost stories hokey, I thoroughly enjoy discussing the ghosts in my hometown with large groups of listeners. I can be found nightly, under the veil of darkness, either on a fluid-stocked catamaran in the harbor or leading people into crepuscular grottos about the town, espousing what I have learned about this vague, wispy subject. Most of the research I discuss on tour—what later evolved into this book and *Haunted Charleston*, both of which I co-authored with Geordie Buxton—came from growing up with some fairly disappointing ghost stories, stories that lacked any sort of real historical bonds or tangible specificity. I became obsessed with revealing "real" ghost stories, not Victorian conundrums that left the reader or listener begging for a meaty detail, be it a scent or a psychological reason for ghostdom.

My quest led me to ask some fairly brazen questions of citizens generally known more for aloofness than candor, especially when discussing the tight fraternity south of Broad Street. I'd anticipated being shunned as if I were asking about some deranged, inbred old uncle who chugged whiskey in the attic. Indeed, many of those I questioned were clearly in denial about their ghosts. But in general, I sensed a secret eagerness in the folks who confided stories of spirits that linger in their homes or places of work. Their enthusiasm made me a believer: too many respectable citizens have offered me too much evidence. Numerous "off the record" tales of aristocrats gone bad, tragic deaths and sad, lonely people came to the surface. I learned there is a profound sense of pride and honor in being able to claim a resident specter, regardless of the desperation or tragedy that inspired a once-living being to become a ghost.

Not everyone is privileged enough to actually see a ghost. Nonbelievers see apparitions often, usually the spirit world telling them to abandon arrogance and realize more exists in this world than football, meat and potatoes, to paraphrase Shakespeare. I know a gentleman who owns a beautiful antebellum inn downtown who swears himself to be completely immune to the possibility of a spectral, spiritual side to history. Yet every once in a while, I'll get a message from this gentleman concerning one of his guests who encountered a foppish Victorian ghost on the edge of the bed. Familiarity encourages sightings. Several longtime workers of the Dock Street Theatre have chanced upon a woman in antebellum attire, believed to be a red-haired woman of the evening, strolling casually through the building corridors. Perhaps the vagaries of chance also allow us to peer into an inexplicable pocket of another world. Or perhaps this has all come to pass because Charleston is surrounded by murky waters that hold more literal and figurative treasure than all of the oceans of the world combined.

To explain what has happened in the waters off Charleston is to bombard readers with so much drama and intensity that they might literally drown in a maelstrom of images. It would be like fishing in the dark to try and capture all the comings and goings of Charleston Harbor, stories that range from the greatest wealth in the world to the lowest depravity in humankind's long, sordid tale. Many great tales of man and the sea, such as Sebastian Junger's maritime novel *The Perfect Storm*, have included Charleston Harbor and its maritime ghosts. Kingdoms have been made in that blue salt concoction; wars, revolutionary and civil, have started here. Many eyes have passed through the slender islands to behold Charleston: some have been glistening with hope; others have been glazed with the fear that comes from being plucked out of your home and thrown into a feculent pine funeral barge—punctuated by shackles and cracking whips—headed into an unknown.

Being a port city, Charleston has been granted a moral duality unlike any other metropolis. Pirates, slave traders and British sailors have stalked and stumbled along the waterfront, confronted by every vice the Bible warns against. The rats that found refuge among the pilings and marsh grass held better ethical ground than many of the two-legged vermin that stepped ashore in hopes of fulfilling every urge their sea-bound lives had not permitted. It was all cheap and plentiful with the devil's seal of approval. All of this took place literally in the shadows of those pious cones funneling stern prayer skyward. The sinners lingered on the harbor wharfs as if on the peel of an orange; the fruit being the Christian families within the city who may have turned their noses up at the sloshing debauchery on the docks, but whose very existence depended upon those rogues with bad livers and tales of sea beasts that grew larger and more fierce with every new port.

Like ghosts, the waters that surround Charleston are dark and mysterious, and the stories have remained, until now, somewhat secret and unseen. These are the stories of a historical Atlantic port city, collected from mariners in vessels and residents who have lived their lives in close proximity to the sea. Like an odyssey, these stories reveal mysteries and wonders of America's most haunted harbor with every turn. Have a look, and begin the voyage into the Holy City's ghostly waters.

Ed Macy

The Pirate Ghost

Stolen jewelry, visions of a man in a white silhouette and droning cries for water late at night have marked the haunting of a pirate ghost at 37 Meeting Street. The lingering spirit has surprised residents in the house and in the back yard, appearing as a blurred image of a man with his arms folded across his chest. He has never appeared to a woman, although he has been heard by at least one interviewed for this book, crying out in a long, desperate call for water as if marooned by his own crew on a dark peninsula centuries ago.

Stories of buried treasure have surrounded the prominent Meeting Street home, with its thick marble steps flanked by twin buttresses, since the eighteenth century. Like most of Charleston's pirate-treasure stories, the bounty never has been found under the house on Meeting or in the back yard. However, the pirate's spirit still lingers, stalking the plot of land where he may have been murdered by his own crew—he was missing from his sloop in the harbor—after they buried their loot on the peninsula centuries ago.

To understand the pirate way of life, one must first understand communism. Cruelty and sadism must be granted an audience as well. Among these seafaring thieves lived a certain nobility, a communal brotherhood confirmed in a catechism of blood. All things were shared, including lesions and diseases; the code of honor meant more than life or gold, and the worst fate, even worse than a flaying over a barnacle-encrusted hull or being eaten by giant sharks, was abandonment. In this culture of skulking confederates, to be ostracized, marooned away from the brethren, meant that a sacrilege beyond penance had been committed.

Pirates had codes well ahead of their days. They had their own form of insurance against loss of limb, a policy that slid down the scale regarding the importance of the limb lost. They shared bounty, and in a Marxist twist, the captain, ever fearful of his ragtag Bolsheviks, took only a small portion more in pay and bedding. These men were superstitious, ever fearful of the leviathan lurking just a few feet below the hull of the sloop, waiting to turn those toothless, sinewy bandits into mincemeat and the ship to splinters. This fear of the unknown and, equally, what they knew to be real, solidified these men as more than family. They had to trust each other or the scales were toppled and all were cast into the blinding depths.

Despite this camaraderie, there lurked purposeful sadism. Captains, fearing the aforementioned mutiny, had to decide the tack to take—not with the wheel and rudder, but psychologically with his men. Like a schoolmaster facing his cretinous charges on that first day of school, law and order had to reign. The edict must be posted, and many captains knew only one way to nail it to the church door: cruelty. Some captains disobeyed the very laws of humanity to garner fear and respect. Carried out were random irrational acts, from floggings to the grisly disemboweling of adversaries. All of this flesh split and blood spilled in the name of order. The crew howled in pain but equally in grim respect for their leaders, men who embraced evil in order to keep the hydra alive.

Pirates who came to Charlestown before the golden age slipped into the horizon were unfazed by the grotesque of sight and smell. For their contemporaries, like the crews of Vane and Stede Bonnet, who were made to "swing," the moments after the hanging were worse than the event itself. In those days, a hanged man did not receive the dignified drop of the trapdoor and the gift of a speedily dispatched neck. In the days when everything smelled like corpses, men set to hang were sentenced to do the hempen jig. A tumbrel cart backed away from the gallows, and the punished dangled in the air, dancing a few feet above the ground in an agonizing attempt to die. Involuntary spasms contorted the swinging man, body fluids and excrement ran down his ankles and he turned purple screaming for the sweet relief of total asphyxiation.

It was not over when the death finally came. The eagle-featured patriarchs of Charlestown saw to it that the bodies remained suspended. Some of the men were coated in pitch to delay the ultimate rot. The elders wanted these men dead, but they also knew the stench and sight of these known decaying forms would serve as stern warning to future lawbreakers. The crabs took what the birds and the heat made fall to the ground.

Everyone was happy in this great chain of being, even the women and small children who, in that day, were used to smelling things that would make the stoutest of moderns gag without cease. Actually, the only ones not happy were the dead pirates, inevitable victims of gravity. When their remains eventually came down— and when that happened, it was usually in pieces—the corpse did not receive the

sanctity of the grave. These men were not buried like the composed corpses of the city fathers, arms crossed in coffins of pine, flanked by slate stones with smiling skulls warning of God's retributive glory. Nor were they buried like their lucky shipmates who died out to sea from disease or battle wounds. (These men were thrown into the deep, where they tumbled for hundreds of stories before setting on the soft, sandy bottom, amid Viking treasures and the indescribable beasts that did not dare disturb these brave carcasses as they settled into that salty slumber.) Instead, the hanged were cast into the purgatorial middle, a place where the superstitious dared not tread: the high-tide waterline. Their bodies were in water and on land depending on the hour, a fate that belied eternal restlessness, much worse than the mortal death received a few weeks before. It was these floating, sometimes bleached, body remnants that ended the reign of pirates. It was not the militia with their endless gunpowder and English sense of barbarity, but half of a grinning, skinless skull sticking out of the mud at what is now the intersection of Meeting and Water Streets, just outside the long-ago wall around Charlestown.

During those glistening days of old, pirate criminals were held for trial at what is now the Old Exchange Building and Provost Dungeon at the end of Broad Street. The dungeon, six feet below sea level, was lined with shackles for the prisoners who awaited their fate among the stench of brine while wharf rats and blue crabs drifted in freely during the nights of high tides. The building, considered one of the three most historic buildings in America because of its role in the Revolutionary War, is a portal to Charlestown's past, where mariners were required to make themselves known at the original Half-Moon Crescent dock that jutted out into the harbor in front of the town's Port-of-Guard.

Just a few homes south of the Water Street spot where angry, tormented bones finally vanished into the asphalt of modernity is the gray mansion with twin buttresses. The modern address is 37 Meeting Street, and because of its age, stature and geographical location, it is occupied by the lingering phantom of what was once a sea-bound family of cutthroats and thieves. His appearance—although usually just a white, blurry silhouette with arms crossed—has given the unspoken explanation of the pirate's dress, or lack of. In a place where modesty existed until modernity, only someone who saw the ravages of the sea would dare walk among such an antebellum treasure shirtless.

This ghost has been seen numerous times and caused a new, proud owner of this impressive home to sell it within one year's time—he sold it because he saw the ghost twenty-seven times.

One eyewitness, a man who grew up at 37 Meeting, remembers seeing the ghost as a child in the 1970s, and the encounters were intertwined with a never-substantiated neighborhood story of buried treasure in the family's back yard. The ghost was blamed for missing jewelry from the boy's mother's powder room on several occasions, having been heard creaking along the stairs while "snooping around" and calling out for water in the middle of the night. The boy, now a man in his thirties, dug up every blade of grass in the yard with his brother in hopes of finding the legendary treasure. Knowing a barrel-chested, marooned criminal from the past bore sentinel duty on the property when the sun hid into the Ashley River persuaded the boys from treasure seeking any more. Innately they knew that the treasure, if it even exists, is what causes that spirit to stay alert for eternity, never to rest in peace like the dead are supposed to. Perhaps the ghost at 37 Meeting was double-crossed by greed and was hanged across from the waterline like dozens before him. His fate was death, but he got much more.

The Mariner's Church

Charleston has been dubbed the Holy City by mariners since its earliest days because of the multitude of church steeples that can be seen from the mouth of the harbor. There are more than eighty steeples reaching to the heavens and nearly two hundred churches in all, resulting in more churches per capita than Rome, Italy. While the plethora of churches alludes to a city built on religious tolerance, there were times of religious intolerance as well during the days of witchcraft and the old British laws.

The heart of the present-day Holy City is home to the Mariner's Church building, with its pyramid roof, iron bell and anchor overlooking the city's historic Market Streets. The first congregation dates back to early Charlestown, when a group of seamen walked away from the First Baptist Church erected on Church Street several decades after its origin in 1682. The mariners built a dissenting meetinghouse across from the First Baptist Church. At the height of the Baptist schism, the mariners' meetinghouse was carried away by the large swells of a fierce hurricane tide in 1752. Religious zealots saw Mother Nature's removal of the mariners' church as a sign of God—a true baptismal cleansing. The mariners were used to a life disrupted by ocean tides, and they hoisted their sinking church onto a boat during the long eye of the monster storm, relocating their sanctuary farther away from the rectitude of the Baptists. Puritanical extremists used the ensuing decade after the great hurricane to crack down on new religious sects, creating a witch-hunt atmosphere that led to a public hanging of accused heretics on the peninsula in 1761.

While members of the Mariner's Church survived the dark times of religious persecution, another dissenting group was not so lucky. A German religious group was eventually hanged in the Lowcountry; group members were part of an eccentric cult known as The Gifted Brethren, who had been banished by Quakers in Pennsylvania for practicing nudity and other "abominations" during their worship service. They moved to South Carolina's Upcountry where they thought they might practice their religion unhampered by authorities.

Captain Han Peter Schmidt was the secular ringleader, known to heal people with herbs, roots and incantations. Schmidt attracted Calvinists and Lutherans who practiced his services with him in the forests near the Saluda River. Worshiping outdoors was routine for most agrarian Germans. An escaped slave from the Lowcountry, known only as Dubard, carefully observed the congregation and joined them with some of his own followers soon after the group settled.

The Reverend Christian Theus from the Lowcountry heard of The Gifted Brethren and wandered into one of their meetings one night in the forest. He found the group at the time Captain Schmidt was trying to raise a dead man from a coffin before the congregation. There were large bonfires all around in celebration of the winter solstice, customary for many eighteenth-century Germans.

The man in the coffin rose on Schmidt's third command. He slowly turned toward the congregation and then gazed with wide eyes at the murmuring members. This was all the Lowcountry priest needed to see.

Theus returned to the Holy City to alert the Charleston militia of the bizarre cult he had observed, and an order was issued to arrest the group. All were captured and put on trial in Charleston where they were sentenced to hang. The executions of The Gifted Brethren were just some of the dark events in a series of public murders that took place on these gallows of Charleston.

The dead bodies of The Gifted Brethren swung slowly for three days in the atmospheric swamp of Lowcountry humidity.

South Carolina has been known to be behind the times socially. It was the last state in America to hear a case of witchcraft, in 1813. After the American Revolution, most of the British witchcraft laws were deleted from young America's law books. The South stuttered for about thirty years before fully claiming independence from the outdated laws of social order.

New England was not the only section of the country where people have believed in witches. Judge David Johnson of Union, South Carolina, who later became the governor, held the 1813 trial of an old woman from Chesterfield who was accused of maltreating, by diabolical arts, a girl residing in Lancaster. The girl testified in court that "Barbara Powers came in and sat upon me, and choked me with great violence. After this she raised me up, converted me into a horse and

rode me to Lancaster…At Lancaster she went through the keyhole into several shops, brought out goods of great value, loaded me with them and rode me into Chesterfield with her booty. Then she rode me to Cheraw, and proceeded in like manner, obtained bags of goods and rode me back to her residence."

At this point, Judge Johnson cut off all further testimony and closed the courtroom. He would not hear the woman's case for prosecution again.

P. Edward Pearson, an attorney from nearby Winnsboro, writing to Dr. Thomas Cooper on April 26, 1837, reflected on the days of witchcraft:

> *In fact, to so great a length did they carry their enmities to a numerous list of individuals, that to relieve the sufferings, it was deemed necessary to give the witches a trial, and if found guilty of the charges alleged against them, to punish with signal severity.*
>
> *In that year a court composed of witch doctors, was held at the house of Thomas Hill, five miles below Winnsboro. Four persons were tried, found guilty and punished by stripes and burning their feet off at a bark fire, so that the soles came off.*
>
> *I can barely remember to have seen one of the sisterhood in the hands of an officer of this court, a poor old German woman, going to the place of trial; and afterwards to have the scars of the cow skin on her arms and shoulders.*

The nocturnal flight of witches has always been held by some as reality, while others have believed it to be demonic illusion. Clerical literature is filled with scholarly discussion on the subject, which resulted in the connection of these flights to the witches' Sabbath and ultimately led to the death sentences of people suspected of nocturnal journeying. Originally, night flying was part of a complex set of agrarian rituals or, more specifically, a farmers' ritual intended to ensure prosperity and fertility to the familial or village community.

People claimed to leave their bodies through bilocation dreaming or meditations, claiming that they were physically able to take on the forms of animals or other people in foreign locations. The Church of England demonized these vestiges of paganism and imposed its point of view, but without succeeding in blocking the nocturnal wanderings of people in outlying areas.

Agrarians would put runes on their houses as guardians of their crops. Many American ancestors were skilled herbalists and healers who placed runes on their chimneys or doors—a practice common for northern Europeans. Rune symbols may have had oaks on them, a symbol of physical and spiritual masculinity, strength and virility. Other runes had pomegranates for fertility and happiness, tulips for peace on earth or whirling stars for movement. These runes, like foreign jewelry on sailors, were unfamiliar symbols to Puritans and caused whole towns to cast their leery eyes on people connected to the unknowns of Mother Nature.

Members of the Mariner's Church were some of the first dissenters of Charleston's early Protestant faiths because they refused to adhere to the taboos of alcohol and public dancing, among others. Mariners, invigorated by the risk and solitude of ocean travel, scoffed at the codes of the land while they drank imported rums and danced into dawn during their first nights back on shore. The conflict between the church and the sea accelerated after the great hurricane of 1752, as other dissenting churches—such as the Unitarian Church on Archdale Street and the Circular Congregational Church on Meeting Street—began to produce their own church dissenters.

Before the great hurricane, in 1745, Chief Justice Charles Pinckney purchased the property along what is now South Market Street. The Market Streets were created by the Pinckneys in a creek landfill project at the turn of the nineteenth century. For a good while, the Mariner's Church site remained at 50 Church Street after the hurricane of 1752. In 1853, the Pinckney family donated the property of the present Mariner's Church site as a place "where visiting sailors of all faiths could worship." In 1915, the current chapel was erected and, the following year, Bishop Leland Guery of the Episcopal Church of the Redeemer consecrated the building.

In 1964, it was decided that the church was no longer needed for mariners and the chapel was deconsecrated. The religious symbols were removed in 1967, and the property was opened as a restaurant. The prayer booths were later gutted and made into bathroom stalls, and the altar was used as a bar—almost as homage to returning sailors. The wildness of the Mariner's Church history has influenced the structure in its present form. At a club on the second level of the church's chapel building, raised cages have recently lined the dance floor—bouncers allow only women to express themselves in the iron-bar cages while people gather for drum rhythms, dancing and drinking.

CASTLE PINCKNEY

Castle Pinckney is no Alcatraz, but the tiny, bushy fort lurking in the middle of Charleston Harbor was once used as a prisoner-of-war camp as well as a site for mass executions. Only seven people have tried to live on Castle Pinckney in the past century. After the death of one of those seven inside a wooden house near the ghostly fort, no one has returned to salvage any kind of life there. The castle's presence evokes fears of the unknown and solitary confinement on a deserted island.

The wooden house on Castle Pinckney where the last death on the island occurred was consumed in a fire in 1967. The fire's origins are unknown, but what survived is the old brick castle next to the house, which is now near two hundred years old. For centuries mariners passing through the harbor have gazed upon the disintegrating marshy isle, originally known as Shutes Folly. It is now a silent, vacant sentinel easily seen from the waterfront, and tourists often mistake it for the nearby famed Fort Sumter.

Castle Pinckney has existed since George Washington commissioned it to be built after his visit to Charleston in 1791, but its story is as little known as its ghosts. Since the McClellan family left in 1935, no one has lived there except for a night watchman.

For a while, the night watchman was the island's only inhabitant. He was enlisted by the U.S. Army Corps of Engineers in the interests of the War Department and was quartered within the walls of the fortress in the 1920s and '30s. The McClellan family, from McClellanville, moved to the island in the summer of 1929. They lived beside the night watchman for nearly six years during the Great Depression. E.P. McClellan Jr., who was seven at the time, recorded his time spent with his two sisters and parents on the island in his critically acclaimed book, *The Ghosts of Castle Pinckney*, published in 1998.

In large part, McClellan's experiences revolved around the phenomena of Mother Nature: eyeing sand lappers and marsh hens, gigging flounder, drinking raisin juice and taking boat rides across the harbor to get to school in downtown Charleston. However, one strange experience took place on the porch of the old house where he lived next to the U.S. Army Corps of Engineering building.

McClellan, following the superstitions of his older sister, was convinced that there was a ghost on the porch. The children's Uncle George had been the last man to die on the island a year earlier in a rocking chair on the same porch while on a retreat to the quiet sanctuary of Castle Pinckney to recuperate from heart problems.

As McClellan described the incident in his book, he was walking out onto the front porch during dinnertime to get the family "flint gun," a phrase they used to describe the bug swatter. McClellan remembered:

> *Now, it was very dark and I was on a mission to get the flint gun. It was resting on the floor beside the chair in which Uncle George died. Just as I reached down to pick it up, my older sister yelled out from the kitchen, "You better watch out, too, Uncle George will get you!"*
>
> *I gasped and gave the flint gun a fling. Instead of going directly back to the kitchen through the hall, I took off like gang-busters around the porch, in the dark, not thinking.*

McClellan then stumbled in the dark—his body flipped over and he landed on his back. Immediately, McClellan thought of his dead Uncle George whose body he had seen hauled away from Castle Pinckney by a dark Charleston funeral-home boat weeks earlier. However, with Shutes Folly's extensive history, the true identity of the spirit world on Castle Pinckney becomes more abstract.

The marshy isle in the middle of the harbor, now almost completely ravaged by storms and tides, was once a two-hundred-acre tract of land. Early colonists drew old maps showing circular formations of oyster shells that may have been refuse heaps for the indigenous coastal tribes. The island is believed to have been a safe haven for the early European colonists when they encountered aggression from tribes such as the Westo, long reputed as cannibals, in the thick forests of the early peninsula.

The island was also used as a place to hang convicted pirates as early as 1717. The hanging corpses were left rotting in the island gallows as a warning to other pirates, such as Blackbeard and Stede Bonnet, who frequented Charlestown during their notorious heydays. In 1746, the island was deeded to a Quaker named Joseph Shute. The Quakers cultivated the land with groves of orange trees. The island remained in the Shute family until 1763.

The American Revolution brought plans for the first fort to be built on the island, following President George Washington's orders in 1794. Shutes Folly had military significance because of its central harbor location, and a fort was built of palmetto logs and mud. It was named to honor General Charles Cotesworth Pinckney, was a Revolutionary War hero. At the time, "castle" was the old English term used to describe an elaborate fort—which the hexagon-shaped wood structure was. The wooden fort was demolished by a large hurricane in 1804 but rebuilt in 1808 with brick. The brick fortress, of which remnants remain today, quartered fifty men in peacetime and more than a hundred when it was fully garrisoned.

In 1855, a navigational light was installed at Castle Pinckney. The fort remained partially armed until the Civil War, mainly used as a city powder magazine. Castle Pinckney's navigational light was activated on and off for harbor pilots until 1878 when a true lighthouse station, complete with a lightkeeper's house, was erected. The lighthouse remained active until 1916. It was completely destroyed in 1938 by a waterspout that blew onto Shutes Folly as a tremendous tornado, skipped across the harbor and then ravaged downtown Charleston.

The day after Christmas 1860, Major Robert Anderson, with his Union forces, moved his garrison from Fort Moultrie to Fort Sumter. This act was seen by Charleston residents as an aggressive act of war. More than thirty men were cleaning and repairing Castle Pinckney under Lieutenant Richard Meade, when, the very next day, South Carolina Colonel John Pettigrew landed on the island. Meade joined the Confederacy with Pettigrew and Castle Pinckney was converted into a prisoner-of-war camp for Union soldiers.

Castle Pinckney housed 130 Union captive soldiers during the American Civil War or, as many die-hard Confederates like to call it, America's "Second War for Independence." By 1864, the prisoners were exchanged, the fort was disarmed and the interior was filled with sand. Only four cannons remained on the island. On February 17, 1865, the Confederate flag was raised for the last time on Castle Pinckney.

During the Federal occupation of Charleston from 1865 through 1879, Castle

Pinckney was converted again into a prison camp. It was used by Federal troops to hold blockade-runners and those still involved with the insurgency against the United States Federal government captive. During this time, the Federal forces executed twenty-five men involved in a mutiny on Shutes Folly, leaving the bloody trail of premature death more congested and the plausibility of ghosts on Castle Pinckney alive.

ECLIPSES OF
PUMPKIN HILL

Some of South Carolina's indigenous tribes looked at death as a spirit's crossing to another shore. In a symbolic sense, the Holy City's harbor has been a safe haven for seafarers escaping a tumultuous world on the ocean, providing a heavenly world of comfort for lost mariners and refuge from the nightmare of hellish sea beasts. The light of fire was kept hanging in a black iron basket off Pumpkin Hill Channel on Morris Island, marking the mariners' passing in and out of the harbor from the Atlantic Ocean.

In 1673, the early colonists asked outgoing mariners to help keep this fire light lit in the iron basket every night on the sandy island. Under the guidance of the light, mariners followed the Pumpkin Hill Channel in and out of the ocean until a more substantial beacon was planned in 1757. The new Charleston Light, named by the English, was delayed because of work needed to complete the steeple on St. Michael's Church. By then, there were nearly a thousand ships clearing the port annually.

The Charleston Light is one of only ten pre-Revolutionary lighthouses built in the British colonies. The original lighthouse tower was shaped like an octagon and stood forty-two feet above the Pumpkin Hill Channel watermark. Once the Revolutionary War began, the colonists extinguished all ten lights so as not to aid the British ships in locating the coast.

The first eclipse of the Charleston Light at Pumpkin Hill Channel, perhaps a symbolic omen, preceded the largest and bloodiest war the virgin East Coast had ever seen. Its light went out on September 15, 1775, when, fearing for his safety, Royal Governor William Campbell fled to the HMS *Tamar*, anchored in Charleston Harbor. The same day, the colonists seized Fort Johnson on James Island, just south of Pumpkin Hill Channel. A small force led by Colonel William Moultrie had captured the fort and they quickly extinguished the Charleston Light. By the next summer, the very first naval battle of the Revolutionary War was fought at the mouth of Charleston's harbor.

The Charleston Light remained extinguished until 1780 when the British lighted it after a successful siege on Charlestown. The British used the Charleston Light to help navigate friendly ships into the seized town. The soldiers held a ball at the Old Exchange Building, above the dungeon where they kept a signer of the Declaration of Independence and a signer of the U.S. Constitution shackled against stone walls in the dank company of wharf rats and blue crabs. Ladies of the town were invited to the ball, but Charleston men refused to allow their women to attend the British ball. The British soldiers instead invited enslaved African and native women. The unlikely mix danced and drank into the wee hours of the night celebrating the siege of the Holy City and the reappearance of the once-darkened Charleston Light. All the while, authors of the new world listened in despondent silence below.

The Charleston Light, a sign of relief to those inbound for nearly two centuries, was eclipsed a second time by Confederates in 1862, marking a blackout on Morris Island that precluded a beach full of bloody bodies. Pumpkin Hill Channel found itself in the midst of the longest-lasting siege of the American Civil War, ongoing for nearly nineteen months. The two bloodiest wars in America's history both have their origins rooted in the eclipses of Pumpkin Hill Channel.

By late April 1861, the Civil War had sprawled out from Charleston Harbor, and lighthouses from Virginia to Texas had been extinguished. In all, more than 150 lights in the South had been blacked out for the war. The Confederacy had strategically destroyed the Morris Island Lighthouse to prevent its use by the Union army as a lookout tower over the harbor. Although the light was eclipsed, the Union knew the strategic value of the location and continued to barrage the Confederate Batteries Wagner and Gregg, just north of the island, until the sea surrounding the lighthouse was tainted red from the wounded bodies of many of the nearly two hundred thousand black soldiers.

In 1981, the bones of nineteen black soldiers were found at a forgotten mariners' graveyard on Folly Beach, just behind the Morris Island Lighthouse, which was rebuilt in 1867 and still stands in the sea. The bones of the lost soldiers, whom South Carolina state archeologists documented as being from the Fifty–fifth Massachusetts and the First North Carolina Confederate Colored Infantry Regiments, were removed and relocated to Beaufort. The old eroded lighthouse stands today like a gargantuan tombstone in the historic Pumpkin Hill Channel, marking the crossing of many souls in and out of the ominous shadow of the Charleston Light.

FACE IN THE FLAG

On the rocky island of the Fort Sumter National Monument, there is a tiny museum within the walls of the fort that holds a prodigy as haunting to many as the Shroud of Turin. Silent in the navy darkness behind the stars of a Federal storm flag is the emblazoned image of a bearded man in a navy uniform. The dark-haired man adorns a soldier's cap and a buttoned coat, facing the defiant city across the harbor that is believed to have indirectly taken his life. Many know the face, weathered inexplicably into the flag's fabric, as that of Union officer Daniel Hough, the first man killed in the Civil War that claimed six hundred thousand lives.

The island fort, made of large rocks hauled by ships to Charleston Harbor from the coast of Maine, is now a major tourist destination. There are bright, yellow harbor flowers that blow in the grass all summer long and halcyon gulls that glide over the brick embankments as they pass in between Charleston's sea islands. In the distance, there is the abandoned Morris Island Lighthouse looming in the sea like a floating tomb. On the other side of the fort, there is the active Sullivan's Island Lighthouse and Fort Moultrie, as well as the historic Rebellion Road channel where ships could float undetected, hidden safely from cannon fire during the Revolutionary and Civil Wars.

Park rangers at Fort Sumter, known for their wealth of facts and historical accuracy, have been dumbfounded on how to handle the questions surrounding the face in the flag. Many have compared the flag to the Shroud of Turin, the most studied artifact in human history. The Shroud of Turin is a centuries-old cloth that bears the image of a crucified man; a man millions believe to be Jesus of Nazareth. A complex chemical reaction between amines and saccharides emerging from the dead body is believed to have left a carbohydrate residue on the burial shroud.

Similarly, Daniel Hough may have been wrapped in the eight-by-fourteen-foot Federal storm flag he was saluting when a freak powder charge from a fort cannon took his life.

The war began on April 12, 1861, at 4:30 a.m. In the dark hour before the war began, Confederate General P.G.T. Beauregard, under pressure from General Wade Davis, sent a letter by rowboat to Union Major General Robert Anderson at Fort Sumter. In the letter, he made an ultimatum: "If you will state the time at which you will evacuate Fort Sumter we will abstain from firing upon you." Earlier, Major General Anderson had moved his men from Fort Moultrie on Sullivan's Island to Fort Sumter, an act local Confederates saw as aggression. It was in this same exact area of dark water at the mouth of Charleston Harbor that the first naval battle of the American Revolutionary War began. Another great war for independence, statistically much bloodier, was about to begin again in this channel where the ocean that divided Charleston from Europe washed into the Holy City.

The ultimatum was denied. Major General Anderson knew his soldiers only had two days of food on the island fort. Edmund Ruffin fired the first shot onto the island of Fort Sumter from Fort Johnson on James Island. A sixty-seven-year-old Confederate from Virginia when he fired the shot, Ruffin was later overcome with great guilt and sorrow at the murderous outcome of the war. Six hundred thousand people had died and, as the starter of the bloodbath, he had lived to see the grave aftermath. He stood alone many moons later, wrapping himself slowly in a Confederate battle flag. He aimed his weapon at the anguish and turmoil of a gruesome war that wouldn't leave his psyche, and he blew his brains into the flag

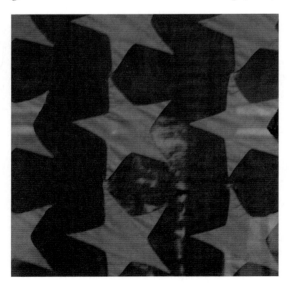

he had put so much faith into.

After Ruffin's first fateful shot on April 12, 1861, the initial bombardment on the fort lasted thirty-three hours. During this time, the Federal garrison flag was ripped by a freak night gale below the fourth stripe to the hoist. This splitting of the flag signaled surrender to Beauregard, who sent men in rowboats over to the fort. Anderson, knowing he was out of food and fresh water for his men, decided to evacuate the island on April 14, after first raising the Federal flag for a final twenty-one-man salute allowed by the Victorian-style militants of the new Confederate States of America. (Later, after the war, Major General Anderson would return in a ceremony to accept the return of Fort Sumter. Had President Abraham Lincoln accepted the invitation to attend the event in Charleston, he would not have been present at the Ford Theater the evening he was assassinated.)

While Daniel Hough and the other men were firing cannons and rifles out into the harbor to salute the Federal storm flag at Fort Sumter one last time, a powder charge from one of the cannons caused an explosion that immediately struck Hough and Edward Gallway. Hough was killed on impact, while Gallway was rushed to the Confederate Roper Hospital on Queen Street where Union prisoners of war would later be held. At the hospital, Gallway bled to death as doctors amputated mangled body parts and wrapped tourniquets on him in efforts to save him. Gallway's dead and dismembered body was delivered by boat to Major General Anderson as he left Fort Sumter.

To this day, nobody knows where Daniel Hough was laid to rest. Major General Anderson did not take his body with him during the evacuation. Archeologists have probed the entire fort island looking for his bones. The closest anyone has come to finding Daniel Hough, the first man killed in the American Civil War, is the haunting face in the flag at Fort Sumter.

THE MEDICINE BIRD

Spirits sometimes manifest in nature in concordance with the risen dead. Through peculiar weather patterns, birds and animals, Charleston's landscape is in a perpetual dance with its ancestors and Mother Nature. The Creek tribe of the Lowcountry, ancestors of the Seminoles, offered their creator, the Breathmaker, ceremonies that involved animal role-playing with alligator hides, deer skins, snowy egret and pelican feathers as well as roseate spoonbills. Their souls were believed to take on the characteristics of the dead animals and birds. There isn't a place in Charleston where supernatural interaction is more evident than Sullivan's Island, where Osceola was buried in 1838. Despite its recent residential popularity, it is still an indelibly haunted land of maritime forests in constant change with the flux of ocean swells and beach winds.

A pelican, said by Floridians to be the spirit of Seminole Chief Osceola, roams the gravesite of his headless skeletal remains on the island. The indigenous seabird, with a pouched bill that can change colors during mating season, is one of the oldest native creatures in the Lowcountry, predating Charleston by the vastness of evolution. After using its sword-like pouched bill to pierce its own chest while in perch, this so-called medicine bird has been seen later in flight, spilling drops of its own blood across the burial grounds of the fierce Seminole chief.

Between a Catholic church known by mariners as the Star of the Sea and the island's still active lighthouse lies the historic Fort Moultrie, where the medicine bird roams. He has been seen in the palmetto trees and myrtle thickets along the rocky beachfront, perched as well on the fort's grassy embankments and windswept parapets. The pelican appears commonplace at first glance, but upon closer examination, fresh blood seeps from his chest feathers as well as stains his lower bill.

The Star of the Sea, built in 1865, is Stella Maris Roman Catholic Church. The Star of the Sea's congregation practices Catholicism where the pelican is an allegorical symbol of Saint John the Baptist, a prophet who preached the coming of a messiah and revelations while washing his congregation over with water. The Baptist, eventually beheaded like Osceola, uses the allegory of a pelican plucking blood from his own heart to feed his flock in relation to Christ's sacrifice on the cross for everlasting life.

The physician who attended the Indian for a throat illness on his last days in the fort's dungeon made a plaster of Paris death mask of Osceola's head. Osceola's skull was removed, and tragically consumed later in New York City by a night fire in a medical museum in 1866. His grave has since been raided numerous times by Floridians who have tried to relocate the rest of the warrior's bones to his homeland. Amid the illustrious history of the fort on Sullivan's Island lies a beheaded reminder of native America, a grotesque tribute to the conquered indigenous tribes along the Atlantic seaboard.

Inside, humid and whispery, the fort is laid out in a maze of arched doorways, dark tunnels, locked cells and powder rooms. The dungeon, where Osceola was kept, is filled with silt mud and broken mortar today. The damp, cold conditions of the dungeon were likely the cause of respiratory problems and throat illness in the Seminole chief. He died in less than a month of captivity at Fort Moultrie.

Cannons still line the walls outside, facing the mouth of the harbor where the British baptized the fort by fire with eleven admiral fleets on June 28, 1776. On that date—now marked annually as Carolina Day—the fort proved to be the hallmark of the first decisive naval victory of the Revolutionary War as the British were repulsed. Fort Sullivan, later renamed Fort Moultrie after the colonel in command on Carolina Day, was saved by the strength of the fibrous logs of palmetto trees. British cannonballs could not break the wood of the palmetto, and the native tree since earned honor on South Carolina's flag. The week after the naval victory, Charlestonians John Rutledge and Charles Pinckney, who are both buried in churchyards on the peninsula, signed the nation's Declaration of Independence from Great Britain. Fort Sullivan was rickety at best when the British tried to invade, but its palmetto logs were replaced by brick masonry soon afterward. It has played a part in later history, gaining prominence in the Civil War. It also served as a training area for amphibious warfare during both world wars in the twentieth century.

With the death of Osceola, Seminole tribes in the East lost their finest leader, and a few months later, the Indians were starved out of Florida. Osceola had organized his people into a campaign of swamp fighting in order to keep from being driven out.

At the height of the Seminole leader's resistance, he entered the camp of General Thomas Jessup under a flag of truce. The general, maddened by public demand for action to be taken against insurgency, seized the unarmed chief and threw him into the damp dungeon of Fort Moultrie. Here the young chieftain's spirit was broken and his body exhausted. His peaceful resignation cost him his life but ended the bloodshed for many; the warrior's death is inexplicably tied to blood spilt on his burial grounds by a pelican, Osceola's medicine bird.

POE

Between the ocean's edge and the Sullivan's Island Lighthouse is the muted dark space of a wind-swept beach where fiction writer Edgar Allan Poe roamed for two years in the late 1820s. Using the alias Edgar A. Perry to escape debtors and a querulous step-father, the young army recruit came to Fort Moultrie when it was an overgrown, mainly uninhabited isle. The ocean air at Sullivan's Island was believed to cure illnesses, and Poe watched the sick arrive by boat to the island's asylum.

Given his leaning toward the darkness of the unknown, Poe was no doubt influenced by his peacetime military years along the harbor. The events in his story "The Gold Bug" are traceable to a real sighting of a pirate ship off Charleston, as documented in the *South Carolina Gazette* in 1735. The two ship crews that reported the pirate ship alarmed the city immediately. The Atlantic Coast's heyday of piracy had been over since the capture of Blackbeard at Cape Fear and the hanging of Stede Bonnet and his crew in Charleston, both occurring in 1718. One of the witnessing ships, bound for Georgetown, was running in a thick fog when the corsair was spotted with a Spanish ship in the Sullivan's Isle channel off Breach Inlet.

The Spanish ship was taking a cargo of gold and silver from Central America to Spain. Her captain made an alliance with the pirate crew in St. Augustine. They agreed to meet off Charleston Harbor, where the gold would be hidden behind Long Island, now the Isle of Palms. The Spaniard was to leave his ship wrecked off the harbor of Georgetown to foil the expecting Spanish government and return to the Isle of Palms in the corsair to divvy up the gold. However, the pirate ship got caught in waterspouts formed by a violent thunderstorm. The twisters drove her crashing into Morris Island where she lost her entire crew. The Spaniards waited in Georgetown after abandoning their ship. The pirates, shipwrecked and dead, couldn't return to pick up the Georgetown crew. The skeleton crew of the abandoned Spanish ship was captured a few days later when they tried to obtain drinking water from a rice plantation near Georgetown.

Poe picked up the old story from the *South Carolina Gazette*, which reported the sighting. "The pilot boat came about, planning to pick up any survivors, but found herself almost alongside two ships that were anchored. One was Spanish, the other the type of fast coasting vessel favored by pirates."

The American author's memory lives on with an old tree on a street named Gold Bug Avenue as well as Gold Bug Island, both in the area where the fictional treasure was found in his story. Poe described Sullivan's Island in "The Gold Bug":

> "This island is a very singular one. It consists of little else than the sea sand, and is about three miles long…It is separated from the main land by a scarcely perceptible creek, oozing its way through a wilderness of reeds and slime. The vegetation, as might be supposed, is scant, or at least dwarfish. Miserable frame buildings, tenanted during summer by fugitives from Charleston dust and fever, may be found."

Orphaned at the age of three, Poe searched desperately throughout his life for a niche. He was expelled from West Point in 1831 after his peacetime service in Charleston and was squeezed by poverty in later years. The poverty made Poe a writer, as he cashed in successful parodies of popular fiction he had written for his own amusement. His fiction was powerful because of the wealth of symbols he used to represent states of inner consciousness—the raven, a windswept tree and the heavy, golden beetle that became his legacy. Poe's style, though hauntingly dark and unorthodox at the time, was refreshing because he did not try to moralize his readers but simply entertained them.

From his fort window, Poe could glance upon the beach and the harbor swells. The fort's strategic point allowed peacetime soldiers, like Poe, to find themselves with little to do. Poe walked across sand dunes along the beach where his subconscious roamed with the seagulls and porpoises. It was here— along the harbor of the city many have called the most haunted in North America—that he gathered material while inventing the early format for the classic American short story.

The Night Rangers

The foggy baritone murmur and heavy steps of these rebel ghosts have been witnessed, but their bodies have never been seen. Locally known as the Night Rangers, they've been heard moving along the Mount Pleasant waterfront down the oak-laden streets of the old village in the darkest hours before sunrise. Pockets of fog shoot out with the sound of their indecipherable conversation; their ethereal breath appears and then disintegrates, only to appear again along their deliberate path.

The haunted walk has been seen ending in the marsh of a wavy inlet by the Atlantic Ocean. It was at this same dangerous body of water, Breach Inlet, between Sullivan's Island and the Isle of Palms, that the Confederate *Hunley* submarine crew was last seen alive. The sounds of voices and movement of humidity trace the same path that the eight men walked every day while training to torpedo a Union ship that was disrupting the local blockade of the Charleston Harbor during the Civil War.

The Confederates submerged inside their primitive submarine on February 17, 1864. They were not seen again until August 8, 2000, when a technologically advanced dive crew lifted the craft from beneath the watermark. They were given a final place of rest in Magnolia Cemetery in March of 2004 before national media attention and tens of thousands of emotional funeral participants. The men's ancient bones—preserved for nearly 140 years by the fine, cold silt mud of the harbor—were revealed one more time to Charleston after the ghostly cadences and murmurs of risen dead were heard for decades throughout the old village.

The sailors' last day above water was bone-chilling and silent. The submarine soldiers of the *H.L. Hunley* barracked in the old village of Mount Pleasant. Led by Lieutenant George Dixon, the crew walked seven miles every morning in the dark to Breach Inlet. Their mission, risky and fearful, had failed twice before, drowning all of the first two *Hunley* crews—including builder Horace Hunley himself in 1863.

The Confederates' desperation to dismantle the Union blockade of Charleston Harbor kept hope alive for the *Hunley*. There weren't any other options left for the failing campaign, begun when the first shot of the war was fired from Fort Johnson on James Island on April 12, 1861. Although the Confederate General P.G.T. Beauregard had grave concerns over the twice-fatal *Hunley*, Dixon urged divers to salvage the ship and pull her back up for a third try. Through rebel eyes, the fate of the Confederacy hung in balance with the third and final attempt for the *Hunley* to undo the Federal government's naval ships.

For a long time, the names of the members of the final *Hunley* crew were as much a mystery as the Night Rangers in the old village of Mount Pleasant. Because the *Hunley* was a venture with close ties to the Confederate secret service, many records were intentionally destroyed at the end of the war to protect the identities of those involved. In 2001, forensic genealogist Linda Abrams began a massive search to discover the identities of the crew pulled from the water just outside Charleston Harbor. The names of the deceased were found to be Lieutenant George E. Dixon, Arnold Becker, Corporal F. Carlsen, Frank Collins, James A. Wicks, Joseph Ridgeway, a soldier named Lumpkin as well as another soldier named Miller.

Beauregard wrote of the third *Hunley* crew's attempt: "After this tragedy, I refused to permit the boat to be used again, but Lieutenant Dixon, a brave and determined man, having returned to the north channel opposite Breach Inlet, materially obstructing the passage of our Charleston, applied to me for authority to use it against the Federal steam sloop-of-war *Housatonic,* a powerful new vessel, carrying eleven guns of the largest caliber, which lay at the time in blockade—runners in and out."

Because the first attempts of the submarine were so flawed, Beauregard was not the only one who doubted its use. From a letter sent to Charleston native Beckie Honour by her husband who was stationed at Fort Johnson come the following lines summing up the submarine's earlier attempt:

> *Sunday morning August 30th 1863, My Dear Beckie: You doubtless remember, and perhaps you saw while in the city the iron torpedo boat which certain parties brought from Mobile to blow up the "Ironside." They have been out three times without accomplishing anything, and the government suspecting something wrong, proposed to them to allow a Naval officer to go with them on their next trial, which they refused. The boat was therefore*

seized and yesterday some men from one of the gunboats was placed in her to learn how to work her, and go out and see what they could do. Just as they were leaving the wharf at Fort Johnson, where I was myself a few minutes before, an accident happened which caused the boat to go under the water before they were prepared for such a thing, and five out of the nine went down in her and were drowned. The other four made their escape. They had not up to last night recovered either the boat or the bodies. Poor fellows they were five in one coffin.

The five bodies of the men who drowned in this gruesome earlier attempt to launch the *Hunley* were too bloated to pull out of the narrow sub's opening; slaves were sent down with hatchets to hack their bodies out. The men were originally buried in a mariner's graveyard that was discovered underneath The Citadel's Johnson Hagood stadium.

The crew aboard the USS *Housatonic* was vaguely aware of the underwater secret weapon of the Confederacy. However, at the time, the idea of a submarine was still abstract and only plausible in theory. Only the most desperate of operations would attempt such a mission of mere suicide. While the Union men looked out aboard their ship, the crew of the *Hunley* sweated over hand cranks that powered a spinning propeller while Captain Dixon manned the dive planes.

The Union navy spotted many porpoises and sharks feeding in the early morning hours around their ship, but when the *Hunley* approached, Union sailors sounded the alarm. They knew the object moving in the dark water below was not a dolphin or shark. It was something more bizarre. The men began shooting frantically at the approaching object with revolvers and shotguns. Bullets bounced off the submarine's cylindrical body as it approached the ship steadfast.

The *Hunley* rammed her long metal spar into the stern of the *Housatonic*. The submarine's spar planted a 150-pound torpedo into the warship. The Confederates lunged forward with the impact, only to quickly back the submarine out as the long detonation rope attached to the torpedo tightened with their departure. Within moments, the *Housatonic* erupted. The dark water between the ship and the submarine quickly illuminated, engulfed in a concussion of fire and exploding debris.

The men in the submarine never returned to Breach Inlet that morning, but the burning *Housatonic* slowly sank down to the ocean floor. The rebel mission was successful, temporarily loosening the blockade of Charleston Harbor. However, the *Hunley* wasn't discovered until more than a century later. Divers were shocked to find the vessel buried deep in the frigid, muddy bottom of the sea, with its hull

protruding at a thirty-degree angle. The submarine had plowed nose first into the black mud, leaving dive crews to speculate that the men may have been knocked unconscious after the torpedo exploded.

The secret of their resting place was hidden and shrouded in mystery for more than 130 years. Since the end of the War between the States, explorers and treasure seekers have scoured the sea around the site of the fallen *Housatonic*, hoping to discover the *Hunley* and her crew. In the years following the Civil War, a reward of $100,000 was offered by the great showman P.T. Barnum to encourage mercenaries to find the lost vessel. The submarine had become a legendary tale, an invisible piece of history, until it was lifted out of the Charleston waters in late summer of 2000 with the bones of the crew still inside.

The origin of the Night Rangers' ghost walk through the old village is unknown. Sewee Indians inhabited the area long before the first white settlers arrived in July 1680. Stories of the ghosts did not begin percolating throughout the neighborhood until at least the twentieth century.

Virginia Lumpkin, a resident on Ferry Street in the old village, has witnessed the haunt on more than one occasion. In an audiotaped interview in September 2004, she recorded her encounters:

> *I have heard these voices of men on several occasions near Alhambra Hall along the Cooper River. I'm one of the earliest risers in the old village because I like*

to walk my dogs before five while my coffee brews. I always get chills when I hear the voices and sometimes I hear just footsteps…I never see anything when I look down the street…and the dogs always start wincing or acting funny. It was last year though that I saw this breathing, like smoke or fog shooting out above the ground below the streetlights. I knew immediately what it was and I knew it was the ghosts. I hid near the marsh behind Alhambra Hall and watched the foggy murmur slowly disappear down the road, heading north.

The old village of Mount Pleasant was the secret training ground for the crew of the Confederate submarine *H.L. Hunley*, and consequently, the souls of these men remain in a perpetual supernatural pattern, still holding out hope for successful secession in the murky corridors of the afterlife.

THE *Comanche*

A Boy Scout sleepover aboard the USS *Yorktown* first revealed the spirits of the Coast Guard Cutter *Comanche* on midnight after Groundhog Day 1987. The *Comanche* account is monumental. There was a mass of apparitions seen in the water during that cold, foggy February night and eighteen witnesses who saw them. No phenomena in Charleston has elicited so much haunting at one time, nor as many witnesses present during the actual sighting.

The USS *Yorktown* aircraft carrier has been anchored along the shore of Charleston Harbor since 1976. The ship rests like a heavy metal chess piece on the Mount Pleasant side of the Cooper River across from Charleston. Its predecessor was sunk by a suicidal swarm of Japanese kamikazes in the Battle of Midway. The original *Yorktown* now rests beneath three thousand feet of water. The USS *Yorktown*, retired after three wars and permanently stationed on the Cooper River, has been an open-air World War II museum marveled at by Charlestonians and tourists alike for decades. It was the largest aircraft carrier ever built upon its completion in 1943. It is also the ship that recovered the astronaut crew of the Apollo 8 after they landed in the ocean after their flight mission to the moon.

Along the side of the great carrier was once the *Comanche*, a lightly armed military Coast Guard cutter used to transport passengers from carriers and to save drowning men caught in the treacherous waters of war. The open, concrete aircraft-landing strip of the *Yorktown* rests several stories above the historic spot of the Coast Guard cutter's haunt. The USS *Yorktown*'s broad landing strip is more than a quarter-mile long and is now an overnight campground for Boy Scout troops visiting from all over the United States.

The first witness who encountered the *Comanche* spirits was found missing around midnight from his Boy Scout Troop camp. His counselor, Art Clawson, made one last round to count heads before he went to sleep two and half hours after the Troop 149 Scouts had retired. Clawson popped his head into each tent on the landing strip and discovered that one of his nine-year-old Scouts was missing. The counselor walked across the long, thick edge of the aircraft carrier, looking for the boy through the windows of model fighter planes and, reluctantly, peering over the side of the ship at the dark harbor below.

The temperatures of February 2, 1987, had been well into the sixty-degree range until sundown. As the Boy Scout troops ate dinner, a cold spring of northeastern air moved over Charleston. After dinner, the group's counselor told maritime stories and war facts about Charleston Harbor and the USS *Yorktown*. He then walked the boys out onto the landing strip. He had the Scouts tie knots to set up their tents while he gave instructions and helped reveal their work with his large flashlight. The chilly night air caused a thick, quiet layer of fog to rise up from the sun-warmed harbor.

Visibility dropped to less than a hundred feet as the dense water clouds floated nearly motionless across the Scouts' tents and the carrier's landing strip. When all the boys' tents were up, the Scouts crawled inside with their sleeping bags. The counselor stepped slowly by the tents as he called out each boy's name to see if each one was in his bag, ready for bed. He poked his head in with his flashlight for confirmation.

It was in these slightly impermeable, chilled conditions that Clawson found the Boy Scout missing from his tent several hours later after the rest of the troops had gone to sleep. Michael Finch, or just Finch, was Clawson's "black bear" Scout, a title he had earned after mastering a knot-tying match with the other scouts. It was around midnight when the counselor looked in Finch's tent with his flashlight. The counselor saw only an empty sleeping bag. Finch didn't respond to his name when the counselor called out into the fog.

Clawson walked nearly a quarter mile along the edge of the landing strip with his flashlight, looking for Finch. He finally found the boy a few minutes later. Finch was standing at the edge of the starboard side of the carrier, in silhouette, in front of the subtle red glow of a harbor light.

The Scout was gazing out over the side of the ship as if he might jump. Clawson put his hand on the boy's shoulder and asked, "Hey, what is it? It's late—we got a big day tomorrow, Black Bear."

The boy didn't move. He kept staring out over the side of the carrier in muted response. The counselor pulled gently on the boy's shoulder, but the boy shrugged him away and continued staring out into the water. Then

Clawson stepped forward to look over the side of the ship where his Scout's eyes were transfixed.

There, in the water, he saw it.

At first there were just a few of them. Soft red glows just below the surface of the dark harbor. Then, many began to appear until the docked *Comanche* cutter was completely visible by red red light rising beneath the water through the fog. There wasn't any sound save for the low, lapping tide on the metal hull of the military vessel.

The glowing red lights intensified slowly and gained in number. In the next three minutes, there were hundreds of lights in the water around the *Comanche*, according to the accounts of Clawson, Finch and the other Scouts who later joined them. The counselor gasped as he pulled Finch back with his hand. The two bumped into the sixteen other Scouts right behind them, all drawn from their tents by the mesmerizing, collective reddish glow.

Clawson compared the peak intensity of the supernatural light with that of a fictional spaceship landing on Earth, except all the red light was coming from underwater. Eventually, each glow faded separately below the *Comanche*. The Scouts questioned one another in the dark and eventually returned to their tents, although none of them slept very well that cold night.

In February 1943, the *Comanche* cutter had left St. John's, in Newfoundland, bound for the army command base at Narsarsquaq in southern Greenland. The crew had originated from Camp Myles Standish in Massachusetts and accompanied five other ships in convoy SG-19. One of the ships was the USAT *Dorchester*, the army's ship whose namesake followed the original naval USS *Dorchester*, named after Dorchester County, South Carolina, as well as the same county in Maryland. The six-ship convoy was soon to pass what had become known as Torpedo Junction—an area of water plagued by Nazi Germany's ability to torpedo up to a hundred Allied ships a month off the North American East Coast.

The Germans had been driven back from Charleston and most of the southeastern coast before the *Comanche* and the USAT *Dorchester* arrived at Torpedo Junction that cold night in 1943. Earlier in the war, German U-boats had hid beside ports and watched the silhouettes of Allied ships moving slowly in front of brightly illuminated cities. Ships would feel safe near the shallow water of the shore as they pressed against the ports from Charleston to Boston, vulnerably lighted by streetlights and channel markers. It was easy for the Nazi submarines to surface at night and wait for a slow, well-lit enemy target.

It was a cold night in the North Atlantic as midnight signaled the end of February 2, 1943, and the beginning of a new day. A German U-boat monitored the slow moving transport of six ships. Shortly before one o'clock in the morning, U-223 fired a torpedo that violently struck the *Dorchester*. German U-223's Captain Karl-Jurgen Wachter fired a second torpedo into the ship before the 902 men aboard could react to the first devastating hit that immediately killed 100 sleeping men in the hull. An explosion in the engine room knocked out electrical power, and darkness engulfed the sinking ship.

Lifeboats floated away before men could get to them. In their state of panic, soldiers overloaded the lifeboats still available, capsizing them into the icy, cold Atlantic. Men scattered to find life preservers and the amber, waterproof safety lights attached to them. The small, red lights began to come on immediately after men fell into the icy water with their life jackets. Soldiers called out to the other ships, "Mayday! Mayday! Mayday!" In fewer than fifteen minutes, the *Dorchester* was almost gone. Heavy frigid waves broke over the railing and tossed men into the near-freezing sea. The *Comanche*, which remained closest to the *Dorchester*, moved in to rescue the drowning men through the coldness. Captain Lee Reynolds directed the haphazard attempts at rescue. Men swam away from the ship for fear of being sucked down by the swelling gorge created by the ship's slip into its saltwater grave. The waves in the sea spread hundreds of other men apart, carrying them screaming in different directions through mist, smoke and darkness. The red safety lights began to fade as men sank lower into the water when hypothermia set in.

Four chaplains, now memorialized for their bravery and sacrifice, in the recent book *Seas of Glory,* were the last men who could be seen standing aboard the sinking *Dorchester,* by the testimony of many survivors. The holy men stood holding hands with their heads bowed in prayer. They stood before witnesses descending in a shared epiphany as they were silently ushered out through a cold passage into eternity.

The chaplains had already given up their life jackets to wounded, drowning men. The silent call of mortal death was near as they left entwined in a prayer, disappearing on a slanted deck without a trace into the cold Atlantic. The brave men were of four faiths. There was Alexander D. Goode, a Jewish rabbi; John P. Washington, a Roman Catholic priest; Clark V. Poling, a minister of the Dutch Reformed Church; and George L. Fox, a Methodist minister. They had listened to the *Dorchester* Captain Hans Danielson's orders to sleep with life vests on because the area was infested with enemy submarines. However, when mass confusion occurred on the ship after the torpedoes hit, many men could not find their life preservers in time. The chaplains sacrificed themselves in giving up their own life preservers to save others.

The *Comanche* and another SG-19 convoy cutter, the *Escanaba*, were able to rescue 245 of the 902 men aboard the sinking ship. However, 15 died later due to wounds and hypothermia. The other men who had drifted off into the distance and submerged into a cold death were left behind unseen, perhaps some still murmuring "Mayday!" softly in the dreary aftermath for rescue.

As the *Comanche* and the *Escanaba* quickly caught up with the rest of the convoy that night, the mist and smoke from the fire shifted. Small, red safety lights could be seen glowing underwater. Prayers were said for the soldiers and chaplains, directed by a Presbyterian priest, Father Gabriel Washington, aboard the Coast Guard cutter. The *Comanche* dared not to retrieve any more bodies that night in Torpedo Junction.

The story of the *Comanche* has become almost legendary through time and peril. Adam Artigliere, a former resident of Charleston, was delivered the story via his grandfather, Lieutenant Robert Anderson, an ensign aboard the *Comanche*. In a military radio show, *The Coast Guard Show*, designed to raise money for the war effort in 1944, the radio announcer, John Reynolds, recaptured Anderson's experience aboard the *Comanche*:

> *Then Anderson told us of the Coast Guard ship* Comanche—*that was his ship—and the job it did that cold night. The sea suddenly became alive with tiny red lights—the life jacket lights that come on automatically. Anderson went overside grabbing life rafts and making them fast. Everywhere he went a huge Negro—that was Charles David—went with him. It was tough, dangerous and unbelievably sad work. Because on some life rafts they would find only one or two live men; the remainder would be frozen stiff in death. On some all would be frozen. Charles Walter David did great work that night. And he kept at it so long he killed himself through exhaustion and pneumonia. And you can't do any more than that—whether you be a mess boy or an admiral.*

Lieutenant Anderson remembered working beside Charles David that night and how David kept at the rescue effort like a manic water bug, even saving the lieutenant's life. Anderson recalled in an interview during the show:

> *That was a tough night, Mr. Reynolds. We managed to drag 94 aboard the* Comanche *and our sister ship got a 123. But many hundreds died. The only consolation is that they died fast, terribly fast. Charles David wasn't so lucky. He was a giant of a man and he gave pneumonia the same fight he gave the Atlantic—but he lost after almost a month. Charles David saved a lot of men that night, and one of the men he saved was me!*

The *Comanche* suffered heavy damage from Charleston's storm of the century, Hurricane Hugo, in September 1989. The cutter banged up against the larger *Yorktown* amid hurricane-force winds and surging tidal waves. In the aftermath of Hugo, the dilapidated *Comanche* was deemed unsafe as a state museum piece at Patriot's Point. It was eventually hauled away from Patriot's Point.

The *Comanche* has since been dropped to make a reef in the ocean twelve miles from Charleston Harbor. Most of the World War II Coast Guard cutter remains underwater today, still carrying its bright mass of red-lit ghosts. According to the accounts of coastal shrimpers, drowned ghosts of *Dorchester* army soldiers still congregate, floating motionless in eddies around the *Comanche* and murmuring through tiny bubbles for their deliverance.

THE TIDE OF DEATH

The Tide of Death, as it has been appropriately called, came by way of an eerie hurricane in 1893 that killed nearly three thousand people in one night. Between Savannah, Georgia, and Charleston, the tempest rampaged with a twenty-foot tidal surge propelled by the winds of a Category 3 hurricane. As the fierce winds of the hurricane shifted back and forth across the islands, the harbor level was reported to drop five feet every ten minutes until the swelling surge returned from another direction with its deadly tide. The Great Sea Islands Hurricane of 1893, best known as the Tide of Death, remains the deadliest in Charleston's history.

Those who have been in the eye of a hurricane have experienced portend. It's that uncanny feeling of stepping foot onto a place known to be haunted. The open sky gives a false sense of comfort as you sense an unnatural presence looming around. Things seem out of place. When the harbor calmly dropped fifteen feet in a half hour that night in 1893, Charleston residents experienced the foreboding eye and the pending arrival of the Tide of Death.

Spaniards first named the present Charleston Harbor on a 1525 maritime map as Baia de San Jorge (Saint George's Bay), but records have not been found of the earliest European settlers who witnessed a major hurricane in the area. In 1964, a tiny crucifix made out of pewter was found while dredging the silt of the harbor's bed. The crucifix was studied and determined to be Spanish, dating back to the fourteenth or fifteenth century. Historians have pondered how the tiny, ornate crucifix got there and if perhaps the owner was cast overboard with it during an Atlantic storm.

The earliest hurricane known of in South Carolina was in 1600. Indigenous tribes passed on oral traditions to the early English colonists. There was a story of the harbor rising higher than the treetops on the day the long-ago hurricane came. Tribes used the maritime forests—now the historic downtown area—as burial grounds, giving away their ancestors to the expanse of the Atlantic. The ocean would rise during the great tidal surges of hurricanes. These enormous tides would wash over the area, collecting buried ancestors and returning them to what many natives referred to as The Great Mystery, the ocean.

Scientists have been studying hurricanes in detail only for about one hundred years. South Carolina's history of hurricanes provides one of the more expansive studies since Central American Mayans first named the huge storms "hurakans." The city of Charleston is brushed or hit at least once every five years and sustains a direct hit between every fifteen and twenty years. One of the most destructive tempests of Charleston's past struck in 1752. The downtown area was nearly completely covered by the storm surge, and shifting winds pounded the area with tidal waves. The Mariner's Church on Church Street was hauled away down Vanderhorst Creek during this storm. Hundreds of people lost their lives in the violent hurricane, but its terror pales in comparison to the Tide of Death.

Supernatural activity and Mother Nature hold the same shock value in South Carolina. Two deadly earthquakes and thirty-seven tropical systems have plagued the city. Every time a hurricane strikes, it becomes clear why the first indigenous tribes of Carolina never chose the maritime forests of the front beaches to settle.

Coastal residents had little defense against the shifting, twenty-foot tidal waves of the Tide of Death. Island houses, all built on wooden posts several feet above ground, caved like card houses. Many homes collapsed, crushing their inmates on the spot; others drifted quickly off with men, women and children stranded inside. In the darkness of despair, Charleston residents clung to the swaying treetops of the giant pines and oaks until the roots gave way and together they were washed out to the reckless billows of the berserk ocean that had sent for them.

The ensuing days after the waters stilled were not very hopeful, especially for people just outside the more solid infrastructure of downtown. Nearly thirty thousand people were homeless. The island victims, with their clothing completely washed away, wandered around naked—or at best, in torn clothing—looking for food and shelter. All vegetable growth was destroyed; all animals, even birds, had been swept away; any fresh water was tainted with salt. The gaunt figure of famine drew near and stared the victims of the barrier islands of Charleston in the face.

Before the inventions of modern communication, coastal residents were given about four hours' notice of a hurricane, if they were lucky. Mariners usually rushed in early from sea to warn port cities such as Charleston. Technology saved thousands of lives when Hurricane Hugo roared over downtown on the fall equinox midnight of 1989. Hugo claimed seventy-six lives, half of those in South Carolina.

The storm fluctuated between its peaks of 160-mile-per-hour sustained winds over the Caribbean to the 138-mile-per-hour sustained winds that circled around its eye when it made landfall. A sixteen- to twenty-foot tidal surge emptied the harbor of boats and demolished coastal property. The counter-clockwise motion of the storm winds and tidal surge wreaked the most havoc just north of Charleston. The Francis Marion National Forest clocked wind gusts of up to 160 miles per hour as the strengthening storm made landfall.

In McClellanville, between Charleston and Pawley's Island, Lincoln High School opened its gymnasium as a shelter. The gym was sixteen feet above sea level, the highest point in the area, and was built to withstand hurricane-force winds. The structure withheld Hugo's fierce winds, but as the tidal surge covered the entire school, the water began to seep into the gym. The tide continued rising until people were forced to swim out of the windows and children were lifted into the rafters to keep from drowning. No one died that night, but everyone in the shelter was frightened to the core.

Every century in Charleston has had its great hurricane, and Hugo captured the attention of the twentieth century. The Tide of Death came in 1893 just before the dawn of communication technology. The fierce tempest would be damaging today, but thousands of lives may have been saved if ample warning was given to coastal residents before the late–nineteenth–century storm struck with its ferocious deadly tide.

THE INVISIBLE FAMILY UNDER THE BRIDGE

On a blistering cold afternoon in 1946, the Robert Alston family of five was believed to have sailed off a broken span of the Cooper River Bridge in their black sedan. After a harrowing descent in the screaming wind, they were reported to have plunged fast and deep into the chilly water below. A sudden gale had caused the ten-thousand-ton *Nicaragua Victory* tanker to drift into the bridge's Town Creek pilings, carving a chunk the length of a football field out of the bridge's span. Other vehicles came within a few feet of the same disastrous fate, and at least one other automobile, the green sedan of the Elmer Lawson family, was reported to have taken the dive as well into the cold abyss.

It was 4:15 p.m. on February 24, 1946, when the accident occurred. It happened so fast that few witnesses had time to describe which cars fell. Most were racing on foot to get back to solid ground for fear that the rest of the bridge was about to tumble. Four eyewitnesses on the bridge claimed they saw two cars plunging off. The crewmembers on the *Nicaragua Victory* also stated that two cars plunged off, one green and one black.

There were more eyewitnesses to the black sedan's nightmarish dive off the bridge than to that of the green sedan. Only after the teeth of a dredging machine's bucket caught the bumper of the Lawson family sedan four weeks later was the mystery partially unveiled. The sedan was green. A fleshless family of five was inside. Where was the black Alston family of five in the black sedan?

The Lawson family was found at the bottom of the harbor, still seated in their underwater car after an entire month, after a busy blue-crab community had nearly scoured their bodies. The Alston family never resurfaced in the harbor after the accident, however, and never fully in the papers, either.

By the fifth day after the accident, the missing Lawson family had a full, front-page spread complete with photographs of all five family members. A small blurb at the end of the article stated that Robert Alston and his family were found safe at home after being reported missing earlier in the week. However, the report was never followed and nothing was ever heard about the family—no celebration of life, no pictures, no statements of relief, only these words in the Thursday, February 28 edition of the Charleston *News and Courier* : "Robert Alston, negro, and members of his family, who had been missing also since Sunday when they went on a motor trip across the Cooper River, have been found safe police reported. They were delayed in returning to the city because of motor trouble."

The short police report about the Alstons who had been missing for four days seemed to satisfy a lot of Charleston readers in those days of Jim Crow laws and racial segregation. It was only after the Lawson family was discovered in their green sedan that questions began to circulate about the black sedan witnesses had reported.

More than a month after the bridge wreck, the paper again reported the possibility of a second car plunging off the Cooper River Bridge, but there wasn't any reference to the earlier police report and the alleged safety of the Alston family. The March 31 edition reported the perspective of the crewmembers of the *Nicaragua Victory*:

> When the men were asked whether anyone on board was injured, all wagged their heads negatively. To questions of injured motorists, they answered by holding up their hands, indicating they thought one car containing five people went overboard. They pointed to the spot where they believed the car went into the chilly water.
>
> Above the noise of the wind, and the water lapping at the sides of the grounded ship, they shouted that they believed that one other car went off the span.

Again and again, the sedan is described as "black" in the numerous reports about the bridge accident. "Charleston green," the actual color, is locally known as a dark color—nearly black. It doesn't appear to have any green at all. However, this description of Charleston green is primarily reserved for the paint on front doors and joggling boards.

Even today, questions still arise among the community about Robert Alston and his family. Who were the Alstons? Who reported them missing? Why didn't the family call anyone after four days of car trouble? There wasn't a celebration of his family's safety if, indeed, they were ever really found safe. The mystery of the Alston family still lingers, perhaps in a black sedan resting in the dark bed of Charleston Harbor.

It may be questionable for drivers to still be using the original Cooper River Bridge in the year 2005. The bridge became eligible to be listed on the National Register of Historic Places for many reasons, including its support beams, which are rusted and nearing a century old. A Confederate who fought in the Civil War was one of the very first to cross the Cooper River Bridge during the opening ceremony.

James Armstrong, the Confederate colonel, snipped the ribbon to open the Cooper River Bridge on August 8, 1929. The old rebel, dressed in a black suit with a bow tie, stood on the same concrete at the foot of the bridge that SUV drivers with satellite digital radio have whipped across. The old Confederacy and present-day modern man are inexplicably linked in Charleston.

The effect of the bridge, with its huge, steel rainbow trestles, on Charleston's history has been astonishing. For decades after the War between the States, Charleston existed in decay and depression. By the 1920s, things finally started to change. Women's suffrage allowed a new spirit to flow into Charleston's social and political life. Northern businessmen, once reluctant to give aid to the bastion of Confederacy, began pumping much needed capital into the conservative city. The increasing traffic from the north side of Charleston put a heavy demand on the limited ferries that ran from Isle of Palms and Mount Pleasant. Bridging the great Charleston Harbor projected great hope for the future of the Holy City. Since the bridge opened in 1929, the face of Charleston has dramatically changed from a deteriorating, ravaged city into a vibrant and prosperous metropolis.

More than six hundred men worked on the great Cooper River Bridge. It was called the most remarkable engineering piece the city had seen since the *Best Friend*, the first passenger steam locomotive, was created in 1830. Surprisingly, only fourteen men died during construction—an astoundingly low number given that the men did not wear harnesses or hard hats while balancing high above the harbor on the steel beams in wind gusts.

The worst tragedy struck on December 1, 1928, when seven men died while constructing one of the anchor piers of the Cooper River span. As the men dug the pier, one end of the caisson hit a pocket of oyster shells, causing the form to sink unevenly. The fifteen "sand hogs," as the workers were called, escaped safely initially. However, when the night shift of ten men and a foreman returned to reset the caisson, it shifted and tons of mud rushed into the working chamber, burying seven men alive. Another sand hog died later as a result of the bends, one worker was electrocuted, one fell from the high trusses and four others died in random construction accidents.

Death followed the bridge after its opening. By 1957, twenty-seven people had died in traffic accidents on the narrow two-lane bridge and ten people had used

the tall bridge for suicidal plunges into Charleston Harbor below. In 1951, a police officer punched and knocked out a waitress who threatened to jump, catching her as she fell.

Decades after the *Nicaragua Victory* incident, a second bridge was built to relieve the bottleneck traffic between Charleston and Mount Pleasant. The bridge was similar in design but included a reversible lane—it was called the Silas N. Pearman Bridge for the chief commissioner of the state highway department. Today, both these bridges have come to the end of their functional life spans. Charleston's salty, humid atmosphere has eaten away the bridges' steel structures. In 1995, state officials reported that the older Grace Memorial Cooper River Bridge attained a rating of only four out of a possible one hundred—the Grace Memorial Bridge became a functionally obsolete bridge long before its deconstruction date was set.

On February 8, 1978, at around 5:30 a.m., a harbor incident involving the *Eurofreighter* came close to the tragic fate of the 1946 *Nicaragua Victory* incident. One of the Charleston harbor pilots was turning the British containership outbound from the North Charleston terminal and had just brought her through the reach between Daniel and Drum Islands. The pilot was completing the final, starboard turn before approaching the two Cooper River bridges. His nephew was piloting the tanker *Gulfseal* inbound on the other side of the bridges with a load of gasoline and lubricating oil. A head-on collision under the two bridges was forthcoming.

The *Eurofreighter* was nearly half a football field tall and three football fields long. Its decks held more than two thousand containers packed with general cargo. Within the thousands of containers were seven containers, the size of tractor trailers, packed with explosives. As the pilot approached the bridge from the north, he had not been told his tanker's bow thruster was on and was drawing much needed power off the ship's engine. Nor had he been told the *Eurofreighter's* main auxiliary diesel generator was undergoing repairs and was useless to help handle any power overload. When a series of mechanical events forced a power overload to fall on the portside engine, the engine shut down. The starboard engine then shut down as well, leaving the drifting ship powerless and in the dark. The distant range light towers that guide the ships, a sort of mariners' gun sight, were the only lights left for navigation in the dark harbor. The ship continued to move, powerless and out of control, toward the two Cooper River bridges. The pilot could see a steady stream of traffic moving over the Silas Pearman and Grace Memorial Bridges. He had no way of stopping or even steering the ship and, within ninety seconds, the *Eurofreighter* was going to knock out the bridge's pilings like matchsticks.

On the other side of the bridge, the pilot's nephew got a call on his walkie-talkie from his uncle. His uncle ordered the rudder hard right on the *Gulfseal* and let go the anchor so that the huge tanker would ground in the mud on the Mount Pleasant side of the river. Aboard the *Eurofreighter*, the pilot called out for Geoffrey Baggins to immediately try and ram his tugboat *Seabrook's* nose against the *Eurofreighter* to avoid disaster. Baggins, a twenty-five-year veteran, anticipated the order as soon as he saw the lights go off on the ship. With fewer than sixty seconds before the ship plowed into the bridge, he rammed his *Seabrook's* nose into the port bow of the containership and piled on all the horsepower. The containership turned, plowing into the pluff mud on Drum Island, a scant few hundred feet from the bridge's pilings.

With the federal government recently allowing plutonium to be brought through Charleston Harbor in the name of national security and corporate markets, the demands on harbor pilots have returned to levels seen in the days of antiquity. In the days of Columbus, pilots did more than just direct ships in and out of the harbor. They accompanied ships on ocean voyages and directed fleets in sea battles. Pilots who failed to compensate for damage done to ships under the laws of King Richard I of England were beheaded. King Louis XIV of France was not so tough. He ordered that pilots who ran a ship aground be whipped and prohibited from ever piloting again. However, if a pilot maliciously ran a ship aground, he would be hung on a mast near the place of the shipwreck. Harbor pilots today are thankful for modern technologies such as wireless communications, power tugboats and radar. The *Nicaragua Victory* and the *Eurofreighter* incidents are historic reminders of the risks pilots face in Charleston Harbor.

The Alston family of the 1946 Cooper River Bridge accident was no stranger to dark mysteries. Just north of Charleston, on the coast of Georgetown, South Carolina, there is an area on the shore of Hunting Beach State Park where the slender figure of a woman has been seen suspended several feet above the water. The woman is believed to be Thodosia Burr Alston, daughter of Aaron Burr, who killed Alexander Hamilton in a pistol duel on a grassy knoll in New Jersey on July 11, 1804. In a sad course of events, Theodosia Alston lost her young son due to malaria while the family was vacationing near the seashore one summer. Because she was so distraught, her husband and father insisted that she go see her father in New York after the death of her son.

Theodosia Alston set sail from Georgetown on *The Patriot* on December 30, 1812. After the vessel reached the horizon, it was enveloped in a fog. The ship disappeared and Theodosia Alston was never heard from again. On the beaches near Georgetown, just north of Charleston, people have claimed to see her ghost suspended above the water. Like the wispy image of a mummy rising out of an underwater sarcophagus, this Alston family ancestor is believed to surface in the midst of the breaking waves. In the slender form of a woman, the ghost levitates motionless close to the edge of the sand—unaffected by winds, fog or the movement of the ocean.

Superstitions of the Mosquito Fleet

*U*p until the 1940s, African American fishermen set out in the harbor in small wooden boats that could be rowed out with the early tides and sailed downwind at twilight, when they would return with swarms of flying insects around their boats. These seamen would venture out as far as thirty miles offshore, many never to return. The disappearance of so many of the "mosquito fleet," as they were called, increased the Gullah superstitions of deadly ghosts and ferocious sea beasts lurking in the Atlantic Ocean in places where no land can be seen.

"Haint blue," a color of paint swabbed onto many boats in the mosquito fleet, was believed to physically ward off the advances of "haint" or haunt forms in Charleston Harbor. Because there are at least ten times as many bodies in the sea than buried on land, the superstitious naturally fear unknown haunts in the water. This color may seem gaudy or absurd to an outsider of this culture, but it is as serious as the dead to those who use haint blue as a deterrent. A haint, in short, is a haunt, but a physical, half-living haunt like a zombie. A dark figure moving below the surface of the water next to a boat may be dismissed as a dolphin or shark by some mariners, but may just as easily be seen as the half-living dead to a Gullah man from the mosquito fleet. The belief in a wide-eyed catatonic stalker swimming around the boat like an amphibious automaton, unaware of its surroundings, was always cause for alarm in places where no land could be seen. Large eyes were painted on the boats of the mosquito fleet to keep watch for lurking evil rising below the surface of the waters.

The disappearance of mosquito fleet boats can be contributed to a number of factors. The most practical explanations involve environmental surprises and human error. Many disappearances happened in an area just off Charleston Harbor known as the Devil's Triangle, or the Bermuda Triangle—one of only two places on Earth where a magnetic compass does point to true north. An area called the Devil's Sea by Japanese and Filipino seamen, located off the east coast of Japan, also exhibits the same magnetic qualities and is known for many disappearances of ships and vessels. In the Devil's Triangle, thousands of large vessels and airplanes have disappeared without a trace.

Every day a number of small vessels called the "mosquito fleet" used to sail out of Charleston Harbor. Slaves who fished for their owners or bought time from slaveholders crewed the mosquito fleet. At the close of the nineteenth century, many Gullah people who lived along the coastal rivers and Sea Islands farmed their own plots. They produced vegetables for local markets and supplemented their diet and income by oystering and fishing. The mosquito fleet grew in numbers after emancipation, and they sailed out the harbor to catch blackfish, porgy, snapper, whiting, trout and croaker. Fishermen sold their catch to hawkers who pushed carts through the streets, shouting out their goods. Porgy fish was considered delectable, inspiring a peddler's chant that was recorded in local author DuBose Heyward's novel *Porgy*. Porgy is also the main character's name in the novel that was made into a famous opera, *Porgy and Bess*, with the musical composition of George and Ira Gershwin. The Gullah chant was heard often on Church and Water Streets:

> *Porgy walk*
> *Porgy talk*
> *Porgy eat wid a knife and fawk;*
> *Porgie-e-e-e*

Fishermen bought one- or two-cylinder engines for their boats in the 1920s in an attempt to keep up with the larger vessels moving into the harbor. At least once a year there would be an explosion, and many times a man would be killed. The engines were dangerous, providing more noise than speed. To keep up with the larger vessels, mosquito fleet fishermen bought old navy wooden landing craft called "buttheads" from the Charleston naval shipyards.

Author Louis B. Rubin Jr. describes the mosquito fleet at Adger's Wharf docks in the 1930s:

> *The trawlers and other workboats that did tie up at the Adger's Wharf*
> *tended to be motley affairs, many of them owned by black fishermen and*

painted with garish colors and odd decorations, including more than one 'eye' to ward off evil spirits lurking in the deep.

The superstitions of the mosquito fleet were integral to the Gullah culture. The local culture is rendered from West Africa, filtered through the Caribbean, coastal Sea Islands and European colonial traditions. Known as Geechee in Georgia, the culture is steeped in the trust of magic to protect from the unknown—fascinating to those interested in the mysterious realms of the supernatural.

CEMETERY BY THE SEA

Though the peninsula of Charleston is a veritable cradle of old cemeteries, fifteen garden cemeteries dating from the 1850s sprawl out on the Charleston Neck along upper Meeting Street. Most of the cemeteries south of the Charleston Neck are charming eighteenth-century churchyards tucked behind the old city's high brick walls. Of the Charleston Neck garden cemeteries, the 120-acre Magnolia Cemetery on the marshes of the harbor, laid out in 1849 on the site of the former Magnolia Umbria Plantation, is the most elegant. Sited on a gentle rise overlooking windswept fields of marsh grass and cattails, the cemetery is home to five dead Confederate generals, fourteen signers of the Ordinance of Secession and a host of living reptiles traversing in and out of its lagoons. The landscape comprises more water than land, and alligators can be spotted sunning themselves between marble tombs and obelisks.

The graves of Charleston's nineteenth-century aristocracy dot the plantation-era landscape of the port where 40 percent of the slaves in British North America entered. The tranquil graves around the watery landscape pay homage to Confederates whose lives were shaped by the system of slavery and the war they waged to keep it. Like the memorial landscapes of Arlington Cemetery or Auschwitz, Magnolia Cemetery stirs deep-seated emotions with the heavy sight of regimented rows of seventeen hundred white tablets marking the graves of Confederate soldiers. Eighty-four of these men were reinterred from the site of the battle of Gettysburg. The Ladies' Memorial Society, fearing the dead bodies of their loved Confederates would not be honored in the Northern battlegrounds where they collapsed, exhumed many of the Confederate bodies from around New England, especially Gettysburg, and shipped them home in piano cases.

In a strange irony that embraces Charleston's truest personality, the remains of the first federal judge to rule the segregationist "separate but equal" doctrine unconstitutional lies within feet of the Confederate markers. The judge, native J. Waties Waring, who died in 1968, mentored Supreme Court Justice Thurgood Marshall. He and his wife lived the lives of outcasts for a long time because of the judge's professional decisions.

One of the reasons for Magnolia Cemetery's creation was to bury bodies away from the city proper to control the outbreak of disease. The literally overflowing graves in the city were believed to be causing certain illnesses such as yellow fever, and the abundant foliage and sea breezes of the Magnolia Umbria Plantation area were believed to reduce contamination.

The Southern secessionist poet William Gilmore Simms, who is buried at Magnolia, dubbed the cemetery The City of the Silent, perhaps in reflection of "The Silent City on the Hill," which is what Cambridge's Mount Auburn Cemetery is called. Mount Auburn, laid out two decades before Magnolia Cemetery, is the likely model for the architect Edward C. Jones who designed Magnolia Cemetery in 1850. With the lushly planted grounds and the visible Magnolia Umbria Plantation farmhouse dating back to 1790 still in use, it is clear that the cemetery was modeled after England's wealthy elite. The English elite first fashioned this type of burial park for strolling in contemplation of humanity's fleeting existence, evoking ideas of man's relative smallness and, most of all, immortality.

The Confederacy's poet laureate, Henry Timrod, wrote about the hardship of the war times and how they affected Magnolia Cemetery. No markers were originally placed on the graves of the first Confederate soldiers buried at Magnolia Cemetery. However, during the Federal occupation following the war, the present marble and granite tablets were culled from stone set aside to build the Confederate state capitol.

In the back corner of the cemetery, within sight of Charleston Harbor, sits the gravesite of Horace Hunley, who put up the money to build the Confederate *Hunley* submarine. Horace Hunley died in an earlier unsuccessful test mission in 1863. Though three different crews of the *Hunley* served, only one saw battle and was recovered from its watery grave in August of 2000. The resurfaced bones of the crew were interred with the remains of the first two crews in the corner of Magnolia Cemetery on April 17, 2004.

Near the *Hunley* crews is a marker that reads, "unknown, Three Bodies, Fort Sumter." Other markers simply read, "Infant." However, monuments also mark the graves of five governors, including Thomas Bennet, three United States senators and two cabinet members. A man on whom many believe Rhett Butler's character in Margaret Mitchell's *Gone With the Wind* was based, George Alfred Trenholm, the secretary of the treasury of the Confederacy, lies six feet under a small marble marker with just his initials and the year of his birth and death.

Magnolia Cemetery—the cemetery by the sea—was founded as a halcyon place, but its graves show that everything but peace existed in the lives of the dead bodies wrought by racial and class tensions. The shift from churchyard burial to secular, garden cemeteries followed a shift in Charleston's society, alluding to an abundance of wealth and sophistication up to the time of the American Civil War. The cemetery's identity is forever stamped by the trail of thousands killed in war, resting silently beside the harbor where the first fateful shots rang out.

The City of the Silent holds some of the most elaborate funerary art of the Holy City. Massive stone crosses, statues and crumbling brick tombs are set against a backdrop of ancient oaks and cattail lagoons whose tides ebb and flow from the vast marshes of the Cooper River. There are intricately carved Gothic monuments and hand-wrought fences reflecting one another across the water, which is draped by weblike, white wooden bridges. There are marble towers decorated in torch flame and rose petal carvings, marble death masks, angels and even a large pyramid tomb made of granite, marble and stained glass.

To get there from the historic Market Streets, you must drive four miles north to an area known as the Charleston Neck.

SEABREEZE HOTEL

The old brick building is still perched on the banks of Town Creek under the long shadow of the Cooper River bridges. Those who checked in weren't allowed to leave. If you were going for a stay at the waterfront "Seabreeze Hotel," you were not to expect bellhops, privacy or a bedtime mint on your pillow. You were packing your bags for a long stay with murderers, rapists, burglars and other thugs. You were committed to the confines of the Charleston County Jail. When the salty breezes from Charleston Harbor blew in and around the building, one readily understood the derisive name given to the jail.

Some places in the port city don't necessarily need ghosts to be haunted. Their creepy history speaks for itself. Such is the case with the Seabreeze Hotel. Many voluntary and involuntary deaths occurred in the building, and perhaps, some souls still linger along Town Creek. However, little could compare to having actually been locked up at night in one of the dirty, overcrowded, dull green cellblocks while listening to the breathing of inmates, the murmur of traffic on the Cooper River bridges and the lapping, dark waves of the harbor.

From 1939 to 1968, hard-line criminals entered the Seabreeze until it became the most overcrowded prison facility in the state. The jail once held a nefarious character named Elmer "Trigger" Burke, a mafia hit man who boasted a brutal slew of murder victims. Trigger checked out of the Seabreeze only to go await his eventual death sentence in New York's high-security Sing Sing prison.

Riots broke out in the county jail throughout the 1960s. In 1963, 168 criminals were packed into the prison that was designed for a maximum capacity of only 125. These unfavorable conditions led to a revolt when 30 men refused to enter their cells from a bull pen and started to roughhouse the security guards. Extra police and firemen from around the city had to be called in to hose the men down into surrender.

Suicides and suicide attempts also blacken the illustrious history of the Seabreeze Hotel. Also in 1963, a seventeen-year-old boy was busted for breaking into a high school at night to steal a basketball and was bound overnight for trial. The boy, bearing his first-ever criminal offense, was lodged with a group of hardened criminals in an over-packed cell. The high-school boy, terrified by vulgar threats and insults, was overtaken by the cold voices of doom. In the wee hours of the morning, while the other inmates had gone to sleep, he hung himself with his own belt out of fear and regret for attempting to steal a basketball.

Immigrant Station was the original name of the symmetrical building when it was constructed in 1912. It was originally built to be the Southern Ellis Island for European immigrants. The federal government planned to process immigrants in Charleston to help relieve the crowds at Ellis Island in New York Harbor.

Shiploads of immigrants from Germany, Holland and the Balkan states arrived in Charleston in 1906, but few others ever followed. The last shipload of immigrants arrived in Charleston on November 4, 1906, aboard the North German Lloyd steamship *Wittenkind*. Immigrant Station was never needed, and the building stood vacant until the 1930s when it was renovated to become an involuntary residential complex, the Charleston County Jail. Balustrades, steel doors, cell rooms and bunker cots were installed to house criminals instead of immigrants.

Poor planning led to the riotous situations in the 1960s. At one point, in 1964, the Charleston Country grand jury called the county jail "totally inadequate" in a May presentment. The grand jury's presentment stated: "Present facilities do not permit an inmate to leave the cell block area for such necessities as meals and physical exercise."

In September, just five days before the opening of general sessions court, the jail's maximum-security cellblock was crammed with 103 prisoners in an area that should have only had 56. Most were awaiting trial or a chance to plea bargain.

The self-professed mafia hit man Elmer "Trigger" Burke was the most notorious to come through the Town Creek jail building. He detested the name Elmer and insisted on being called Trigger. It's likely that the debut of the Looney Tunes character Elmer Fudd struck a sensitive chord in the ruthless mafia man. Producer Chuck Jones's release of *Elmer's Candid Camera* in 1940 depicted an egghead cartoon character with a bulbous nose, eccentric clothing and a milksop voice. The Elmer Fudd character became hugely popular in the 1950s during the same time Burke became known around New York mafia circles for his brutal killings.

Burke began his career in crime with petty robberies with his older brother Charlie. Both were reared from the poverty-stricken Irish ghettos of New York. Burke was sent to reform school in 1941 but had his sentence cut short for joining military service. Burke returned to New York, and throughout the late 1940s and early 1950s, he rented himself out as a hit man for hire, specializing in machine-gun killings. He was sentenced in 1946 for robbing a liquor store at gunpoint and served two years in New York's Sing Sing prison.

During Burke's stay in the big house, his idol and older brother Charlie was gunned down in an underworld mafia shoot-out. Burke swore vengeance, although he never knew who killed Charlie. Upon his release from Sing Sing, Burke hunted down a man he suspected and blew the back of his head off with a double-barreled shotgun without the man's confession. He went back to his business as Trigger the hit man and began charging $1,000 for a standard syndicate murder.

Burke was known for his fierce and wildly out-of-control temper. He once shot a bartender in the face for interfering in a fistfight he got into at a local Irish pub. The bartender made the mistake of protesting when Burke kicked his already unconscious victim in the head.

In 1954, Burke was hired by the mob to travel to Boston to kill Joseph "Specs" O'Keefe, one of the brains behind the million-dollar Brinks Bank robbery. The mob had figured that O'Keefe would cave to police pressure and tell who was behind the robbery, so it was essential for the criminals to kill one of their own men. It would also mean more loot to split between the hyena-like thugs.

Burke found O'Keefe in a housing project and calmly chased him around for a half-hour, letting off dozens of rounds from his machine gun until he finally shot him in the leg. Burke then toured around Boston for the next week, enjoying the city's historic landmarks and coffeehouses while thinking he had successfully killed O'Keefe.

O'Keefe filed a complaint against Burke to the police for attempted murder while he was recovering in a Boston hospital. Patrolman Frank Crawford found Burke in the Back Bay section of Boston. Burke was confined to the Charles Street jail but escaped. He moved south to hide in Charleston over the course of the next year.

In Charleston, Burke met his friend Thomas Francis "Duke" Connelly Jr., the getaway driver in a $205,000 robbery of the Woodside branch of the Chase Manhattan Bank in Queens, New York, in April 1955. By this time, Burke was wanted for murdering a bartender and for questioning in his possible involvement in six other murders.

Connelly and Burke were known to be regular customers of the YMCA health club where they mingled with some of the city's influential and prominent citizens. They also were known to shag at Issy Sabel's club on Market Street. The two bought shoes at Henry Berlin's on King Street. Berlin remembered telling Burke that he thought the man was crazy for wearing such small shoes. When he related the story to Federal Bureau of Investigation agents later that year, one agent told Berlin that he was lucky he hadn't upset Burke who was known to off men with far less provocation.

On June 27, 1955, Duke Connelly and his wife disappeared. The suspicion is that Burke killed the two in order to get the loot from the Queen's bank heist. The Connelly couple has never been found, and Burke never spoke about their disappearance. There is a legend around Isle of Palms that $90,000 was buried by Connelly on the island or one of the islands accessible by the Intracoastal Waterway. Much real estate has been dug up in search of this loot, although the money has never been found and the Connellys have never resurfaced.

FBI agents arrested Trigger Burke in late August 1955 on the corner of Erie and Center Streets on Folly Beach. It was on Folly Island that Burke was found hiding near his rented cottage while waiting on a bus into downtown Charleston. Connelly, if still alive, may have turned him in under a witness-protection program. Only the secret investigative circles of the FBI know the details of how the fugitive was eventually found, but it is fact that Burke checked into the Seabreeze Hotel on Town Creek where he stayed in the maximum-security cellblock.

Burke was convicted of murdering bartender Edward "Poochy" Walsh and sentenced to death following his stay in the Charleston County Jail. He was electrocuted on January 9, 1958.

The metallic rattle of keys and the dull clank of doors still echo through the building as maritime lawyers and other tenants now occupy the recently renovated complex. The Seabreeze Development Company converted the building in 2001 for office rental space, incorporating its colorful history into a sort of prison motif. Original steel bars still line the hallways, bathrooms and other areas as saltwater breezes encircle the building. The ghosts of the old county jail remain highly visible on the banks of Town Creek and Charleston's historic maritime twentieth century.

Knock of the Earthquake Boy

Earthquakes, unlike hurricanes, don't have seasons. A visitor may turn to the Weather Channel to know when to avoid winds of 160 miles an hour from the Atlantic, but there aren't any absolutes in a city historically known for being a grab bag of disaster.

A British boy visiting family friends at the Bull-Huger House in the late summer of 1886 was fatally surprised when he stepped outside to see why his hosts' mansion was shaking. He was standing solid on the stone top of the front steps when the ornamental edge of the roof's ceiling collapsed on him.

The Bull-Huger House's ornate drawing rooms rattled like stormy seas but were not destroyed during the great earthquake that killed the young visitor. The main drawing room, which extends across the front of the entire second floor, is the same room the boy left when the shock was most violent. A dim glow has been seen moving through this drawing room and a ghost has returned to knock on the front door, wanting desperately to be let back in.

House residents and passers-by have been puzzled by its phantom occurrences. For the most part, the ghostly knocking belongs to late summer nights. The knocking was also heard during an earthquake that surfaced on Veterans Day 2002. It came on the evening an undersea quake fifteen miles off the coast rattled the Lowcountry.

The Prioleaus, who were hurrying down the street to a cocktail party on South Battery, paused when they passed the front door of the Bull-Huger House at 34 Meeting Street. A quick tapping sound caused them to turn and look back at the door. They saw no one standing there. Mr. Gaston Prioleau dismissed the knock as child's play, which, supernaturally speaking, it was. He whisked onward down Meeting without waiting for his wife, Marla.

Then the knock came louder. Mrs. Prioleau stepped away from the front steps to look up the side of the mansion. Mr. Prioleau stopped and looked back at his wife. The Prioleaus both felt a subtle shift in the sidewalk beneath their feet.

The mansion, once thriving with family life, was dark and empty except for what looked like a dim security light in the second-floor drawing room. The dim glow illuminated the roofline ceiling of the Bull-Huger House. Mr. Prioleau returned to his wife as they listened to yet a third knock. He grabbed his wife's arm as they hurried away, glancing back suspiciously over their shoulders at the old mansion.

The undersea quake that night in 2002, only 4.2 in seismic strength, was strong enough to send Charleston Southern University research scientists into a collective frenzy. Men and women spent the next day calculating the potential damage if an unannounced major earthquake, such as those of 1698, 1812 and 1886, thunderstruck the peninsula.

Two fault lines squeeze the city. There is one whose epicenter rattles the town of Summerville twenty miles north, where a visible crater from the earth splitting in 1886 still raises eyebrows among passersby. The other fault line has its strongest quakes fifteen miles off the beaches of Seabrook Island, south of Charleston.

In 1698, Charlestown resident Afra Coming, wife of Captain John Coming, writing her sister-in-law, Elisabeth Harleston, in Dublin, Ireland, said of a Charleston earthquake: "Ye country full of trouble and sickness. Ye smallpox &c. followed by an earthquake and ye burning of ye town and loss of cattle do from ye hard winter."

Although the earthquake of 1698 may have been considerably strong, the damage from this earthquake was probably not much as there was little to destroy in those days. There is no record of the severity of the shocks.

Mrs. Coming died the following year, but from her and her husband, Coming Street in Charleston and Comingtee Plantation on the Cooper River received their names. Comingtee was their plantation home and Coming Street was part of the land they gave as glebe land for St. Philip's Episcopal Church.

On February 7, 1812, another large earthquake was recorded in Charleston. Because the city had grown considerably, more accounts of damage were found than Afra Coming's 1698 account. Charleston reportedly shook several times within a few hours as chimneys fell and houses cracked. The next morning, a lunar eclipse occurred as Holy City residents watched in the dismal aftermath. The eerie creaking of the woods permeated as palmettos, oaks and pines balanced their trunks on their torn roots.

The masonry ornamentation that made up the roof's edge of the Bull-Huger House also fell unexpectedly in 1812, just as it would in the earthquake of 1886. Unfortunately, there had been a man named Francis Huger standing on the stone front steps of the Bull House, as it was known then. The house had already become famous, since it had been rented by the British Royal Governor Lord William Campbell in 1775. Campbell escaped from Charleston revolutionaries that year when he fled out the back garden of the house in the middle of the night, down Vanderhorst Creek, now Water Street. He had seen war emerging in the streets and escaped on a boat that waited to take him to the HMS *Tamar*. After the royal governor's departure, Captain John Bull bought the house from the attorneys of an Indian trader, George Eveleigh. Historians have been unable to agree whether Captain Bull, who is said to have named Bull Island, named the home or whether his widow did. That night in 1812, however, Francis Kinloch Huger, who in 1794 had tried unsuccessfully to rescue Lafayette from the Castle of Olmutz, was nearly killed when a part of the bull's-eye in the roof fell. The parapet landed on him and fractured his skull.

His cousin, Mrs. Huger, who took upon herself the responsibility of refusing to allow him to be trepanned for fear of permanent injury to his brain, may have saved the man's mind. In 1812, surgery on the skull was an uncertain operation. Huger's mind was saved by Christian Science, and he lived to buy the house in 1818. He eventually became a lieutenant colonel in the U.S. Army, and he joined in welcoming Lafayette inside St. Michael's Church down the street from the home.

On August 31, 1886, one of the great earthquakes of U.S. history occurred in the Holy City. Only the great San Francisco earthquake of 1906 and the Good Friday 1964 earthquake in Alaska (which created tsunamis in Japan) rival the one in Charleston. The 7.6 magnitude quake killed 110 people, and 90 percent of buildings endured significant damage.

Initially, the quake was perceived as a barely perceptible tremor. A roaring sound "like horses running over frozen ground," as one resident recalled, bellowed through the city. All movable objects began to shake and rattle. Then the tremor became a rapid quiver. The quiver lasted for nearly a full minute while thousands of brick chimneys crumbled off roofs. The heavy thud of piazzas and church steeples crashing into the streets could be heard as Charleston residents held one another, ran and screamed. The stucco in walls cracked and floorboards popped up and down. Everywhere slowly became dangerous and unsettled. Homes and buildings collapsed entirely. There were seven additional shocks over the next twenty-four hours.

More shocks continued over the course of the next months. Men who were skilled in the art of brick masonry flourished in the aftermath of the wrecked city. Over fourteen thousand chimneys had been destroyed by the quake.

The cities of Columbia as well as Augusta and Savannah, Georgia, also experienced major damage. The earthquake affected more than five million square kilometers and included distant points such as New York City; Boston, Massachusetts; Milwaukee, Wisconsin; Havana, Cuba; and Bermuda. All or part of thirty states and Ontario, Canada, felt Charleston's 1886 earthquake.

Homes on the lower part of Meeting Street received considerable damage during the great quake. Four homes down from the Bull-Huger House, the William Mason Smith House at 26 Meeting Street was severely damaged. All four walls of the house needed extensive repairs. On the official report that listed each building on the street, in the category titled "What should be done to make it safe," the engineer reported, "rebuilding it."

Although many families around the lower peninsula flourished during the Victorian times of the late 1880s, most had neither the means of repairing their homes without slave labor nor the materials. Most Charleston homes and buildings were hastily reassembled with the use of long metal rods that were twisted together to form beams to keep the floors and walls together. Charleston's populace remained camped in vacant lots, public squares and the middle-of-winter streets in tents improvised of carpets and blankets while reconstruction work occurred.

Many priceless landmarks were destroyed or badly damaged, although St. Philip's Church, to which Mrs. Afra Coming had given the glebe, remained standing, its steeple battered but upright. Hurricane Hugo magnified the hidden earthquake damage in St. Philip's steeple when the storm roared through town with winds of 138 miles per hour. St. Philip's church steeple is held together today by several metal beams to keep it from falling onto Church Street. Around Charleston, St. Philip's is known to hold the oldest congregation in the Holy City, dating back to 1680. The prominent congregation has been known to stand firm in its religious ways, leaning ever so slightly to the right, and the leftward tilt of the steeple caused by natural disasters is believed to hold the oldest congregation in karmic balance. The floor beneath St. Michael's Church steeple, where the St. Phillip's congregation originated in 1680, is several inches lower than that of the main church due to the earthquake.

Thirty-six prisoners escaped from the Charleston city jail through a fissure in the wall. Six shots were fired by the guards, preventing a jailbreak, as the inmates made a dash for liberty. Water and gas lines broke throughout the city as scattered fires flared up. People were restrained as they became frenzied with religious fright. Meeting, Market and East Bay Streets were wrecked. Railroad service was paralyzed on account of twisted rails.

John B. Gadsden was at a political meeting at Summerville High School, near the epicenter, when the massive earthquake struck. Summerville residents periodically saw trees fall down in local swamps during tremors weeks before the great quake. Many figured the alligators had become disturbed, eating the trees out of the swampland. Gadsden was in his mid-twenties and was a bookkeeper for a Charleston business when the big one hit. Here is an excerpt from his account that has been kept in the South Carolina Geological Survey:

[L]*ike a stroke of lightening, exactly at 9:51 P.M. I was sitting near a large double-door, and was at the point of rising to my feet when it came. I was seized by an irresistible force which seemed to carry me whither it would. The floor, ceiling, walls, window-frames seemed to be dancing, struggling, and doubling, as if to break themselves, and the whole house appeared to be (no other words can express it) galloping down the hill. The terrible roaring and rushing noise, which filled the air, did not so much frighten as awe me, and I trust that never again may the feelings I experienced during the shaking of that building come to me or mine.*

While the disturbance was at its height, no human voice or cry could be heard, and falling chimneys and walls were not noticed until afterwards. Standing as I was in the doorway of the hall, I was taken up into the air and thrown by the struggles of the mass of men behind me down the steps which led from the hall; but, strange to say, was not in the slightest degree hurt...to my own knowledge and that of others the force of gravity was considerably lessened; for I seemed to fall slowly as a feather or any light substance would, and yet I fell from a distance of from six to seven feet.

The young British boy would likely have lived if he never left the Bull-Huger House the night of the great earthquake. Many lives were saved by the cumbersome rituals of Victorian times in 1886. Although many thought to leave their shaking homes immediately, the custom of dressing in many layers kept them inside when they jumped out of their beds that night. The ghostly knock on the front door of the mansion is a reminder of Charleston's supernatural world and the ever-lingering presence of the Lowcountry's powerful seismic fault lines.

Up in the Air:
Charleston's Truly
Unexplainable

Millions of planets can already be detected by the magnification of telescopes. Of these millions of planets, there are myriad more stars similar to our sun. Within the entire universe, there is vast space encompassing things not yet manifested, along with the distinct possibility of life beyond Earth.

Charleston's history of unexplained phenomena goes beyond the universe of ghosts—and above. In the last year of novelist James Fenimore Cooper's life, he published a short story about a mysterious artillery-cannon sound along the East Coast, which has come to be known as "the Seneca Guns." The loud booms still rattle the windows of Lowcountry homes, and scientific researchers have differed widely in opinions over exactly what causes these sounds. But as if the occurrence of the Seneca Guns weren't bizarre enough for Charleston, since the 1970s, there have been frequent unidentified flying object (UFO) sightings within the vicinity near the U.S. Navy and Air Force bases.

On the night of Valentine's Day in 1977, an auto mechanic named William Herrmann reported a claim to Charleston County Deputy Sheriff Pike Limehouse that a bright light abducted him in North Charleston and dropped him in a rural field on John's Island three hours later. In the 1980s, there were several more sightings, with photographs, and on July 6, 2003, a Summerville woman recorded a UFO on her video camera for approximately three minutes before it vanished into thin air. Most recently, on November 21, 2004, while walking their dogs at Sunrise Park on James Island, a couple reported a low-flying "moving constellation" of seven objects.

The oldest television news network in the Southeastern United States, WCSC in Charleston, investigated the Summerville woman's 2003 videotaped sighting. WCSC's reporter interviewed a university astronomy professor as well as the

National Weather Service, but no explanations completely resolved the report of extraterrestrial life humming around the Holy City.

On June 19, 1953, announcer Charlie Hall spoke the magic words: "Channel Five is now alive." The televised broadcast crackled into thousands of darkened homes all over South Carolina, eastern North Carolina and Georgia. Rooftop antennae sprouted all over the Southeast to tune into the new miracle of television. Some folks, who didn't even own sets, climbed up on their roofs to put an antenna up just for social status.

The broadcast, produced with a nine-man staff and two cameras, was a reminder of the advent of local radio twenty-three years earlier. On May 14, 1930, WCSC radio aired for the first time in Charleston. State Senator Cotesworth P. Means was the master of ceremonies for the opening radio show and also opened the first television show for WCSC-TV. WCSC dedicated the station "to the services of God and man," and Thomas P. Stoney and the Spirituals Society were on hand to sing music. Shows were conducted in accordance with film programs drawn from major television networks and broadcast through a 440-foot high tower (twice the height of the Holy City's tallest church, St. Matthew's Lutheran) on the corner of Alexander, Charlotte and East Bay Streets.

John M. Rivers Sr. was the original owner and president of WCSC. He applied to the Federal Communications Commission for a channel allocation after being involved with WCSC radio for decades. He gathered his main staff from WCSC radio, including station manager Roland Weeks, and pioneered a new world—the first VHF television station in South Carolina.

Being the only VHF station in South Carolina, Channel Five obtained programs from four networks: ABC, CBS, NBC and the now-defunct Dumont systems. Art Carney, Bob Hope, Milton Berl, Loretta Young and Arthur Godfrey were all seen on WCSC in the early days. The most popular syndicated shows were *The Lone Ranger*, *Boston Blackie*, *Flash Gordon*, *Lassie*, *I Led Three Lives* and *Sea Hunt*. Senator Joseph McCarthy's hearings were the first form of reality television as Charleston residents watched him crumble from public power in the privacy of their own homes.

Viewers were faithful to the television until *The $64,000 Question* game show revealed how deceptive television could be. Until then, those who advertised on television saw enormous response by getting the benefit of appearing like a best friend at one's dinner table asking for money. But *The $64,000 Question* was a popular program where the contestants were told the correct answers while locked in a secret vault as they tried to win the titled prize. When a government investigation probed the depths of the deception—the fact that the unknown contestants were really known by the producers and coached the correct answers in advance—television lost its innocence to viewers when the show was canceled because of internal corruption.

Local television networks have helped television regain its integrity by attempting to report the most up-to-date, accurate news. The videotaped sighting of a UFO in Summerville in July 2003 might make any television viewer suspicious. But WCSC Live 5 News reporter Harve Jacobs presented an objective investigation while showing the actual footage of the UFO from the video camcorder of the Summerville witness, Linda Moore. Here is the actual transcript that originally aired on WCSC Live 5 News on November 25, 2003, at 6:15 p.m.

WCSC News Anchor 1:
>A strange sight in the sky catches the eye of a Summerville woman.

WCSC News Anchor 2:
>And her quick thinking caught the images you've never seen before on tape. Harve Jacobs tells us what experts think this identified flying object could be, and then you decide for yourself.

[Clip of actual footage shown]

Linda Moore:
>Oh my God...

WCSC Harve Jacobs:
>It's 8:30 on the night of July 6th and a Summerville woman can't believe what she's seeing through her camera lens.

[Clip of actual footage shown again/voice-over]

Moore:
>Oh man, this is too cool...

Jacobs:
>Something she's never seen before, an unidentified flying object. *[Goes to sit down for interview with Moore.]*

Moore:
>As I kept watching it... um, I was like, "Wait a second, this is something else."... I'm pretty much a skeptic and...uh, I always say I have to see it to believe it. Well, I definitely saw something, but I can't say what it was or what it wasn't.

[Clip of actual footage shown again/voice-over]

Moore:
>That is something all right...

Jacobs:
>Could it be a flying saucer over Summerville?

Moore:
>I didn't see any green or gray men, I just saw an odd object in the sky and I taped it. I don't think it was an airplane out of focus. I think it is definitely an unidentified object, and I've yet to find an explanation for it.

JACOBS:

> We wanted to find an explanation, too, so we showed the tape to College of Charleston's Astronomy Professor Terry Richardson.

[Shows each expert viewing the footage/voice-over.]

PROFESSOR TERRY RICHARDSON:

> I've seen lots of UFOs, well they became IFOs— identified flying objects— once we figured out what they were.

[Voice-over]

JACOBS:

> In this case, he says this object most likely was a weather balloon. *[Goes to sit-down interview while watching the footage.]*

RICHARDSON:

> It's the right time of day, and from these pictures, it looks to me as if it was some of the same qualities.

[Voice-over]

JACOBS:

> But the folks at the National Weather Service say it couldn't have been one of their weather balloons. *[Goes to sit-down interview while watching the footage.]*

STEVE RENKEN OF NATIONAL WEATHER SERVICE:

> The closest thing I've seen to it is the research balloon from Texas. The research institute down near Houston, where they sometimes release these research balloons that go way up into the stratosphere. And that's the thing, that's what it reminds me of most.

[Voice-over/shows images of www.roguesighting.com Web site]

JACOBS:

> Linda wants even more opinions; she's set up her own Web site and posted frame-by-frame photos of the unidentified flying object she saw. *[Goes to sit down with Moore.]*

JACOBS:

> Do you think you'll ever find an explanation for it?

MOORE:

> No, probably not.

[Shows each expert viewing the footage/voice-over.]

JACOBS:

> It looks like the mystery over Summerville won't be solved anytime soon.

[Clip of actual footage—strange object shown in slow motion. Close of the report with reporter Jacobs in the WCSC news studio.]

The South's oldest newspaper, the *News and Courier* in Charleston, has not escaped documenting reports of UFO sightings in the Lowcountry. "Witnesses 'Just Froze' As Eerie Form Flew By" is the headline derived from the Monday, July 17, 1989 edition of the local newspaper.

As the newsprint explains, an eerie UFO was sighted a quarter mile from the Federal Aviation Administration tower and the Charleston Air Force Base. The reported UFO was an "enormous" dark object, according to witnesses. Many local residents are aware of the C-5 and C-17 air-transport aircraft flying in and out of the military port city of Charleston.

In 1989, President George H. W. Bush had the naval base in North Charleston 100 percent operational. During the July week the UFO was reported, the stealth bomber made its debut, proving itself as the military's new undetectable engine of injury. High winds and scattered showers caused some structural damage to homes around the area the night of this report. This is an excerpt from the *News and Courier* article: "Jim Pierce, the Federal Aviation Administration supervisor at the Charleston airport tower, said that although the controller on duty early Sunday didn't see anything, he did receive numerous reports of UFO sightings about 1:30 a.m., some of which came as far away as Tybee Island near Savannah, Ga."

Nothing ever came of the report. In fact, in a very brief article in the paper the following day, the sightings were dismissed as Soviet rocket debris.

In *Contact with Reticulum*, authors Wendelle C. Stevens and William J. Herrmann describe Herrmann's alien abduction account in Charleston. According to their book, on February 14, 1977, Herrmann, a local photojournalist and mechanic, left his Charleston home at around 9:30 p.m. in order to get a better view of a bright light that was hovering over electrical pylons near the Charleston Air Force Base. He soon found himself staring out into an empty field on John's Island fifteen miles south of his home. His read his watch, telling him that three hours had passed. Deputy Sheriff Pike Limehouse was called to question Herrmann and found the man in an excited, distressed state; Herrmann believed he had been abducted.

Herrmann's experience with extraterrestrials continued after that night. The next year, while he was driving his car to church, he saw a UFO shoot across the road. He stopped his car and watched the large metallic saucer follow a peculiar triangular flight pattern. Herrmann succeeded in shooting a number of good quality photographs of the UFO.

Although, he believed he was alone while he took the photos, the following day he received a call from the Charleston Air Force Base asking that he turn over his photographs to the base's information officer. The person on the phone identified himself as Tim Osborn and said the base was collecting information on a "phantom" aircraft.

Herrmann met with a man who identified himself as Tim Osborn at the Mills Hyatt House Hotel in room 520 where he was immediately given a polygraph test. The man was dressed in black, just like the notorious governmental men in black, and repeated that he was Tim Osborne. Herrmann was questioned for between sixty and ninety minutes. Herrmann handed over several photos but kept the rest for himself.

Several days later, a man named Tim Osborn called again and said he wanted to come down from Johns Hopkins University in Maryland to question Herrmann. When Herrmann replied that he'd already met the man Osborn at the Mills House Hotel, the real Tim Osborn on the telephone told him that he had met an imposter and advised him to always ask for identification when anyone asked him about his UFO photographs.

✝HE SEΠECA GVΠS

James Fenimore Cooper was the first American novelist to accurately describe the peculiar phenomena known as "the Seneca Guns" that occur regularly around Charleston. The mysterious booming sounds have been theorized to be alien aircraft, geological plate shifts, air pressure changes, Civil War ghost battles and remnants of atomic-bomb testing.

The sounds echo around the Lowcountry mainly during the day. They are ghostly sounding but very loud and real. The sounds have been so loud as to rattle windows and frighten people into calling local authorities. The mystery is that nobody has ever been able to figure out just what the sounds are.

In his short story—one of the few he ever wrote—"The Lake Gun," Cooper describes the sound from the perspective of Seneca Lake in New York, where the East Coast phenomena got its name. Cooper describes the occurrence in concordance with the Wandering Jew, the medieval legend of Ahasueras who mocked Christ on his way to the cross and was condemned to walk the Earth until Judgment Day. It is around these two eerie entities, the Wandering Jew and the Seneca Lake guns, that his short story is developed. Cooper describes the lake guns as so:

> *It is a sound resembling the explosion of a heavy piece of artillery, that can be accounted for by none of the known laws of nature. The report is deep, hollow, distant, and imposing. The lake seems to be speaking to the surrounding hills, which send back the echoes of its voice in accurate reply. No satisfactory theory has ever been broached to explain these noises. Conjectures have been hazarded about chasms, and the escape of compressed air by the sudden admission of water; but all this is talking at random, and has probably no foundation in truth. The most that can be said is, that such sounds are heard, though at long intervals, and that no one as yet has succeeded in ascertaining their cause.*

Whether the sounds are completely supernatural has never been determined. Cooper, best known for his work *The Last of the Mohicans*, wrote his short story in the final year of his life. The sounds are as eerie and alive as they were in 1850 when "The Lake Gun" was published. The curious booms continue in accordance with man's rural development of the eastern seaboard—they continue around the Lowcountry as nature's incessant daytime haunt.

The Sibilant Siren

As long as men roll off the sea, there will be certain necessities ready to greet them and welcome them back from the dangers of the deep. Rum, grog, ale, mead, wine: depending on the time and the ethnicity of the sailor, there was always a tankard ready to be emptied. Sometimes the libations were needed because of a physiological addiction, raging chronic alcoholism attributed to bad habits, rowdy ports and medicinal purposes. Other times, a normally steadfast and sober salt would drink to forget something from the waves. Whatever the case, the barkeeps and tavern owners cared not. They knew the men of the sea had very little else on which to spend their wages. As long as there was a sea, there would be thirsty men ready to drink themselves into the oblivion of infancy, the maternal ocean long since past.

Something else called sailors ashore, much like the sirens called the Argonauts onto the calamitous rocks off the shore of that mythological patch of sand in the Aegean: the flesh. Women of loose virtue have set up shop on the banks of villages, the docks of towns and the ports of cities since the beginning of time. After the quenching of the sea-wrought thirst, the urges of the flesh had to be gratified, and the bawdy districts always stood within the shadows of the ships' masts.

Charleston was no exception, but rather an exemplar of vice. Her brothels, bordellos and whorehouses ranged from grimy mattresses in back alleys to grandiose antebellum properties, gilded with the finest comforts of the day. There were different districts about town. Some were recognized by the red light burning in a window or above the door, the universal symbol of prostitution. Others were so well known and publicly accepted, they stood firm in the path of mainstream commerce, with broad daylight transactions done under the noonday shadow of ecclesiastical justice.

Madam Grace Peixotto ran a grand place on Fulton Street that serviced men of wealth as well as men burned by the salt and sea. Confederate sympathizers and Union occupiers crossed paths in her velvet-lined hallways during the early years of Reconstruction. It was said when this beloved matriarch passed, her funeral was markedly more prominent and well attended than those of the time's deceased aldermen and mayors. Grace Peixotto's place was a cathedral dedicated to vice in a city filled with wooden pagan altars. One of those dens of iniquity still stands as an apartment building next to one of the nation's first municipal fire stations.

As the call of duty signals with the sirens of the men's transport, something as ethereal as fire itself is awakened in the nineteenth-century, brick carriage house across from the firehouse. The ghost, never reported seen, has been heard whispering in either of the two, small enclave bedrooms on the second floor. Other sounds heard by residents have been the deep inhalations of a woman, soft echoing sounds of passion. Light footsteps have been heard on the stairs and windows have suddenly opened during hot summer evenings.

One resident interviewed said he felt the overwhelming sense that someone was looking at him downstairs from the stairwell. When the resident looked up at the stairs, nobody was there. Soft footsteps were heard climbing the stairs and the sibilant sound of a dress flowing around the ascension.

Nobody knows who among the past living that the spirit belongs to. She could be as dated as the tiny carriage house itself, built of brown bricks, wood and mortar next to the firehouse in the nineteenth century. The carriage house became the Southern Air Motel in the 1950s. While few can presume that it was still used for its original purpose, it closed after the two-story brick firehouse, built in 1887, continued awakening night guests with its sudden sirens. Today, those sirens still awaken one revenant, whispering sleeper of the house.

EPILOGUE
LETTER TO BOTH SIDES

Last year, I died when the rebels came to town. It was not my intention to be ushered into afterlife prematurely, just on the cusp of my thirtieth year, nor did I foresee my departure coming. It was a clumsy, drawn-out death over the course of a hectic week, ending with a sole legion among the ranks carrying a Dixie flag past me through Magnolia Cemetery and, posthumously, a film that wrenched the sunken Confederacy out of the jaws of obscurity.

I took a job with a group of videographers to document the burial ceremony of the CSS *Hunley* submarine crew. The dead Confederates, hidden inside their primitive sub since 1864, made their way into everyone's personal lives that April week. Ten thousand Civil War reenactors flooded downtown Charleston in honor of these once-forgotten men. Uninformed tourists settling in to see the charm of window boxes and sweetgrass were rudely awakened from their bed-and-breakfasts to a hurly-burly army clad in burlap. Piercing rebel yells echoed throughout harborside streets and the ballast-stone alleyways. I caught one couple from Toronto, Canada, on tape dodging a wad of tobacco chew, spat out by a fake soldier waving his iron musket. The CSS *Hunley* ceremony served as a platform for a free-for-all against the sensitive boundaries of political correctness, and I saw it all through the wide-angle lens of a Sony DSR-500 camcorder.

The Confederate funeral was a domino in a recent series of events that has put South Carolina on top of America's national attention. In 2000, fifty thousand people marched in protest to the rebel flag flying on the rooftop of the state capitol building. African American activists urged people to boycott the state entirely. Even after the death of South Carolina's one-hundred-year-old Senator Strom Thurmond in 2003—a politician who holds the Senate record for the longest filibuster to civil rights, jumping political parties when the laws passed; the same man who ran for American president on a "Dixiecrat" segregationist platform in 1948—the Confederate flag still waves gallantly today at the entrance to the capitol building; it's as if the War between the States never really ended.

The job began with a daylong round of interviews with the ancestors of the submarine crew on April 12. The organizers of the funeral week, including state Senator Glenn McConnell, were honorable sons of Confederates themselves and thought it polite to have the Confederate funeral ceremony on the exact calendar day the American Civil War began, rather than the day "The Great Unpleasantness" ended. The choice in date was a symbolic hope for resurrection of the gentile South to rise again, a sort of renewal of a club of the misunderstood. The week proceeded with emotional lectures at the Charleston Museum and cannon firing on the grounds of the old Citadel. It ended with a four-and-half-mile, ten-thousand-person march whereby the caskets of the eight dead men were carried to the final burial ceremony at Magnolia Cemetery on the marshy banks of the harbor. Initially, I had no idea whom I was working for when I was hired for this fateful job. Working in the Charleston film industry is much like being employed in a traveling circus. If and when you get a job, you get few details about what you are about to do and, more often than not, you have never met the out-of-towners you are about to work with. I'd worked a grab bag full of film jobs from videotaping the sports try-outs for the film *Radio* in Walterboro to holding a long boom mike for a Los Angeles, director Jordan Brady (*The Sweet Science*), who—for three straight days on the set—never removed his dark sunglasses while his creative juices flowed into the making of an Angus-beef burger commercial. More often than I'd like to admit, I have worked as a "gofer" in productions. I have not been a rodent, per say, but a gofer, meaning I've been sent out to go fer coffees, go fer videotape, go fer finding an extra electrical outlet, and on and on—a gofer.

When the local producer contacted me for the *Hunley* documentary, he said I'd be working alongside the great cameramen of CNN, FOX, ABC, CBS, as well as many other established media network companies. This was all true—they were all there on the first day of interviews at the old Charleston naval base to film the descendants of the dead submarine crew. I set my equipment up right next to Jerry Gilford from CNN in Atlanta, Georgia, who had just returned from shooting combat shots from a tank in Baghdad, Iraq. However, my press pass bore none of these prominent media names when I planted my tripod down to document the interviews. The yellow pass around my neck that got me into the media-only area read "the Sons of Confederate Veterans." Needless to say, I received leery-eyed glances from the other media people. Some stared hard at my pass, as if they'd encountered a Forrest Gump, nodding slowly at me while they set up their cameras. "Who in the hell are the Sons of Confederate Veterans?" I was afraid someone would ask. And, finally, someone did. Dumbfounded, I responded gruffly that they were my video team and "we" were making a professional documentary regarding the true *Hunley* experience—the *real* story. The explanation got me though the first day, but when I met the director at the Charleston Shotgun Club that night, a place rumored to have been the sight of Klan rallies in the 1960s, I pressed him hard with my own questions.

The Confederacy has always been a sensitive subject for me since growing up on James Island where Edmund Ruffin fired the first shots onto Fort Sumter. When my father returned enlightened from a grueling navy-medic service in Vietnam, he became the first to treat a black patient at the longtime segregated Roper Hospital, once a Confederate hospital, in downtown Charleston. He caught hell for it from other Charleston surgeons at the time but was later rewarded for his philanthropy when civil-rights laws pushed all the way through public Charleston by 1970. I was weary that I was getting roped into a group at the *Hunley* funeral that would ebb the social progress Dad helped forge years earlier.

I asked the director of the documentary—a bright, fast-talking man with a strong drawl—what the Sons were all about. As if I'd asked him to expound on Copernicus and Aristotle, he went off on the origins of the Confederacy like a windup doll. All his fast talk was relevant and greatly intriguing, but I knew I had to ask specifically what drove this group's passion. "Do you believe America would be better off today if the South had won the Civil War?" I interrupted.

"What Civil War?" he shot back in a growling drawl. There was nothing civil about the way he said "Civil War," either. "Civil War? There was no Civil War."

"Well something happened in the 1860s—some real big-ass war—and hundreds of thousands of people died," I said.

"That was the War for Independence," he corrected me.

"That was with Britain," I retorted. "Seventeen hundreds—"

"Yes, it was with Britain. Them wig-wearers. The war in 1861 was the Second War for Independence. America lost. Britain won." End of subject, the man seemed to imply as he walked off toward the barbecue.

I was silent for some time, digesting his perspective. There are many social groups, such as the Sons of Confederate Veterans, who still feel the pain of loss in a cause their grandparents were told was right as religion. The group claims to have more than forty thousand members and growing. The Vietnam War, like the Civil War, will trouble American generations to come. The wars in Iraq and Afghanistan are opening wounds irreparable for generations of Arabs and Americans to come. Dixie has climbed out of darkness since Vietnam and racial segregation ended, and to many, love has flourished, leaving a social fabric in the South that has come to fascinate people rather than threaten them.

Knowing where we were, the stories I'd heard about the Charleston Shotgun Club, I walked back over to the director. I tapped him on the shoulder and asked, "What about slavery? Abraham Lincoln freed the enslaved."

The director spat chew on the ground near the outdoor grill where we were standing and turned to me. "Friend, are you trying to get yourself killed? We were trying to free those slaves long before Lincoln still had his. We tried to abolish slavery to prevent the bloodshed, don't you see? Lincoln wouldn't listen. Six hundred thousand dead! All for what? Segregation didn't end until the 1960s—not 1860s! Slavery was a way of life—as abusive in as many ways as life is to many folks today! The war was about land and power—wars always are. We were our own nation of farmers here in the South. Rich in resources from the Blue Ridge to the coast and back to the Mississippi. Longer seasons, more sunshine, more crops with a social system to yield those crops and feed everyone. Look at the land now. Look what Yankee industry has made of the land now! And why do we need all of this military—to prevent farmers from pitchforking for land?"

Those who came to represent at the final ceremonial day for the Confederate crew were generally soft-spoken and solemn. On camera, some mimicked the eloquence of Thoreau while others carried a wicked *Deliverance* back beat to their demeanor. There were a few among them whose talk was so marbled they might as well have come to Charleston via a medieval time machine. The director speedily pointed out that these types of people exist in every society. He again pointed out that I'd be lucky if I didn't get myself killed.

And so it was to be on this final day of the ceremonies when the enormous funeral march toward Magnolia Cemetery finally settled in the hot sun for the remainder of the afternoon. Everybody who was anybody with any oral skills began a long list of final farewells before an omnipresent, curious television audience. As I filmed a group of women crying beneath their black veils, I looked up to see a flag of the red-and-blue Saint Andrew's cross rippling out of the corner of my eye. The enormous flag was moving through the still ranks of spectators gathered for the interment.

That was when I saw him, the man who blew away my former self. I thought I was fixed in my social quagmire of Southern identity. But yet he advanced slowly through the still congregation. This African American man in a rebel military uniform quietly stepped through the huge crowd of silent onlookers as he progressed across the lawn carrying his flag. His eyes were attentive like a warrior; his face was as determined-looking as a painter. He reared from Alabama and had made the trip down to Charleston because his great-great-grandfather was a freedman who had been in the maritime business with Lieutenant George Dixon's family before the Civil War. His ancestor had fought to preserve a way of life that was everything to him, and the man before my camera lens was paying homage to his *Hunley* submarine crew connections like so many of those gathered to see these once-lost men receive final burial.

If my video camera hadn't been firmly placed on my tripod, I just may have dropped it into the wide creek that runs through the Confederate cemetery. The day's sad parade had proceeded along East Bay next to the mountainous battery plantations houses built on the backs of African and Native American labor. Many of the participants had joined in shooting cannons on the Saint Andrew's cross pathways in front of the old Citadel built in response to an alleged slave insurrection by a freed black ship carpenter, and here the funeral procession ended in Magnolia Cemetery, an area steeped in Confederacy. As hundreds of rebel flags passed through town on the way to the cemetery, I saw many blacks huddled in Charleston single houses, fearful, some hollering in disgust over the pain of slavery, the torture that had occurred on this land, the conflict, the heavy burden, so easily identifiable with the old South.

But here was a man who came to celebrate a bond of human endurance that connected eight men lost at sea with his ancestry who had crossed over those same white-capped waters off Charleston Harbor. This sole legion came to acknowledge the fanatical bravery of those lone men in that cold, tight corridor of their primitive submarine, with only tiny candles and a map to guide them in the dark, knowing that only seven of twenty-eight crewmembers had survived the peripatetic coffin. These men, forgotten for nearly a century and a half, had been passed over by the swiftness of time and tides, shackled in a forgotten legacy by a lack of modern archeological tools. As the sun beat against the kneeling man's face, his dark eyes glistened with respect to the solemn lowering of the eight crewmembers' caskets. And here I was in the cemetery crossing over to the other shore, witnessing the final interment through my camera lens and capturing a parallel: free at last, we were all home and we were free at last.

Geordie Buxton
2004

BIBLIOGRAPHY

(Charleston) News & Courier, "1698 Earthquake in City Recalled," August 24, 1934.

(Charleston) News and Courier, "Ship Cuts Gap in Cooper River Bridge During Gale, Car Plunge Reported : 100-Yard Section Falls as Vessel Drags Anchor," February 25, 1946.

(Charleston) News and Courier, "WCSC-TV On The Air Today," June 19, 1953.

(Charleston) News and Courier/Evening Post, "Castle Pinckney Is Destroyed By Flames," December 23, 1967.

"The Coast Guard Show," broadcast on 1130AM June 4, 1944.

Cooper, James Fenimore. "The Lake Gun." New York: George E. Wood, 1850.

Gordon, Michael E. "Patriot's Point will review plans to sell *Comanche*." *(Charleston) News and Courier,* December 7, 1989.

Heywarad, DuBose. *Porgy.* 1926.

Hicken, Patsy. "Channel Five is Now Alive." *charleston* magazine, November 14, 1977.

Irby, Laurens H. "Most Public Officials Agree County Jail Sorely Needed." *(Charleston) News and Courier*, October 25, 1964.

Johnson, Skip. "Harbor Incident." *(Charleston) News and Courier/Evening Post*, January 22, 1984.

Kropf, Schuyler. "Plan to sink *Comanche* under fire." *(Charleston) News and Courier*, December 6, 1991.

Lake, William G. "Witchcraft in South Carolina." *South Carolina Magazine*, June 1952.

Lecouteux, Claude. "Witches, Werewolves, and Fairies: Shapeshifters and astral doubles in the middle ages." Rochester, VT: Inner Traditions, 1992.

Locklair, Bernie. "Harbor Pilot: An Exacting Trade." *(Charleston) News and Courier/Evening Post*, April 11, 1972.

McClellan, E.P. Jr. *The Ghosts of Castle Pinckney*. North Charleston, SC: Narwhal Press Inc., 1998.

Reyna, G. Jr. "Witnesses 'Just Froze' as Eerie Form Flew By." *(Charleston) News and Courier*, July 17, 1989.

Save the Light Foundation. www.savethelight.org

South Carolina Geological Survey. "First-Hand observations of the Charleston Earthquake of August 31, 1886, and Other earthquake materials." Columbia, SC: South Carolina Geological Survey, 1986.

Wales, Ken, and Poling, David. *Sea of Glory*. Nashville, TN: Broadman & Holman Publishers, 2001.